Black Anarchism and the Black Radical Tradition

Moving Beyond Racial Capitalism

By
Atticus Bagby-Williams & Nsambu Za Suekama

Edited by
Shannon Fauwkes with Howard Waitzkin

Daraja Press

Published by
Daraja Press
https://darajapress.com
Cantley, Québec, Canada
2022

© 2022 Atticus Bagby-Williams and Nsambu Za Suekama
All rights reserved

ISBN: 9781990263323

Cover design: Kate McDonnell

Moving Beyond Capitalism —Now! Series editors:
Howard Waitzkin & Firoze Manji

Library and Archives Canada Cataloguing in Publication

Title: Black anarchism and the Black radical tradition : Moving beyond racial capitalism / by Atticus Bagby-Williams and Nsambu Za Suekama ; edited by Shannon Fauwkes with Howard Waitzkin.
Names: Bagby-Williams, Atticus, author. | Za Suekama, Nsambu, author.
Description: Includes bibliographical references.
Identifiers: Canadiana 20220414963 | ISBN 9781990263323 (softcover)
Subjects: LCSH: Anarchism. | LCSH: Anarchists. | LCSH: Black people—Politics and government. | LCSH: Anarchism—United States. | LCSH: Anarchists—United States. | LCSH: African Americans— Politics and government. | LCSH: African American political scientists. | LCSH: Capitalism— Social aspects.
Classification: LCC HX833 .B34 2022 | DDC 335/.8308996—dc23

Dedication

To all of the Black anarchists, revolutionaries, rebels, anti-authoritarians, outsiders and outlaws. I hope you find this book helpful in navigating everything. Black anarchists find ourselves caught between many hostile forces, even among those who claim to be our 'comrades.' Hopefully, this project makes you feel less alone and more empowered to take action for Black autonomy. - Atticus

And this is also for all the ones who could fly, for the ancestors, and laborers, and elders, wanderers, caretakers, builders
warriors, crafters, witch doctors
farmers and hunters, gatherers
rioters. And for the pirates and the runaways, the maGes and street queens, the hood niggas and single mothers, and all the wild things Man cannot tame.
all those forgotten
and unprotected, all those who cannot love
or live as themselves freely, all those who fought
and died for our freedom all our people,
wherever we are, and our Homeland
and our planet, all beings,
even those who aren't human
and all people treated as less than human; all those whose brains
work different and whose bodies
work different too; all those in prison
and on the street.

And for all power to all the people:
from below, through the margins,
in self determination.

The original of the words above appeared in the text "Mapping Our Legacy: The Narrative of Black Freedom Struggle" by Afrofuturist Abolitionists of the Americas

Acknowledgments

Thanks to everyone who worked on the project. There's a lot of people I can thank. Ultimately though, the project was a product of community. Y'all know who y'all are. I'm trying not to give the FBI the names of any of my comrades. I'll try to make sure I get copies sent to all of you, though!
- Atticus

I am glad to see that there has been a second wave of Black Anarchists since 2015, arriving on the scene. I support the rights of all Black Anarchists to build their movements, and I defend the rights of Anarkata. I don't agree with everything in the book, but that is immaterial. This is an excellent book and well-written.
— **Lorenzo Kom'boa Ervin**, activist and author of *Anarchism and the Black Revolution* and *The Progressive Plantation*. During his over 50 years as an anarchist, Ervin was a member of the Student Nonviolent Coordinating Committee (SNCC), the Black Panther Party, and Concerned Citizens for Justice, and he founded the first Black anarchist federation in North America, Black Autonomy.

This revolutionary book reveals the political power of "stretching" the classical anarchic tradition to critiques of racial capitalism. Bagby-Williams and Suekama deliver an accessible, thought-provoking analysis of two waves of Black American anarchism: that which arose from 20th century politics of Black liberation and the later reanimation of anarchism triggered by 21st century killings by American police. The authors layer deep class criticism with insightful case studies not just to retrace a history of Black anarchism, but to make a compelling argument about the diversity of thought that influences the radical tradition. With this book, the historical and continuing contributions of feminist thought, queer activism, and anti-colonial struggle to the movement are made clear. Readers will learn that Black anarchism has not died due to "progress," but rather proliferated in light of the American tragedy that is capitalism, imperialism and brutal, carceral control. This book has nuance. Read it now!"
— **S.M. Rodriguez**, Ph.D., Assistant Professor of Gender, Rights and Human Rights, London School of Economics, and author of *The Economies of Queer Inclusion: Transnational Organizing for LGBTI Rights in Uganda*. Website: www.smrodriguez.com

A necessary and accessible historical analysis of the often overlooked Black anarchism. Bagby-Williams and Za Suekama demonstrate that any revolutionary movement truly committed to a post-capitalist world must constructively engage with this Black radical tradition.
— **Toni Harrison**, Black Canadian writer, community organizer, and host of the podcast *Actually Existing Socialism* (https://podbay.fm/p/actually-existing-socialism).

Thank you for sharing the pamphlet. Once I started reading it I could not put it down. It was refreshing to learn about the different texts, approaches and experiences of Black anarchism. What stood out the most for me was the inclusion of feminist and queer perspectives moving away from the ableist heteropatriarchy lens. In an era where movements are advocating for the abolition or reform of oppressive systems, this text helps in reflecting and reimagining what new inclusive systems may look like. It also makes an important analysis that highlights the complexity and diversity in Black anarchism, which is essential if we are to confront the white savior complex and complacency in addressing inequities and dismantling racial capitalism.
—**Tinashe Goronga**, medical doctor and public health leader in Zimbabwe; one of the global coordinators of EqualHealth's Global Campaign Against Racism affiliated with the international Social Medicine Consortium; and Mandela Washington Fellow 2022.

Contents

Dedication	v
Acknowledgments	vi
1. "Anarchists, We See You"	1
2. European and North American Anarchism Confronts Black Radicalism	5
3. The Evolution of Black Anarchist Politics	19
4. The First Wave of Black Anarchism	22
5. The Second Wave of Black Anarchism	39
6. Conclusion: Toward Black Autonomy	49
References	51
About the Authors and Editors	54

Chapter 1:
"Anarchists, We See You"

In May 2020, the United States experienced an explosive racial reckoning, unlike anything the nation had seen or felt since the 1968 riots that occurred in response to the assassination of Dr. Martin Luther King, Jr. Only a few months into the COVID-19 pandemic, the Minneapolis Police Department's Third Precinct went up in flames when members of the Minneapolis Police Department brutally murdered 46-year-old George Floyd. The images went viral due to the quick thinking of a Black teen who stood witness to the execution that day. Parts of multiple cities around the United States and eventually the world became engulfed in riots as rebellion in Minneapolis spread, leaving a path to anti-racist resistance in its wake. Anti-police graffiti was thrown up on walls in many cities, even as monuments to white supremacy, embodied largely by statues commemorating "heroes" of the Confederacy and colonial powers, were defaced and pulled down.

Minnesota Lieutenant Governor Peggy Flanagan, in the days following the burning of the Third Police Precinct headquarters, viewing the large-scale destruction of property and seemingly coordinated direct actions taking place all around Minneapolis, exclaimed, "There are anarchists. There are people burning down institutions that are our core identity." After tweeting a video of a random white man wearing all black at a protest, former President Donald Trump echoed Flanagan's sentiments, ominously captioning said video with a simple, "Anarchists, we see you." The specter of anarchism, conjured and fed by mainstream media and U.S. politicians, lingered over the continuing protests. In many cases, anarchists were blamed as the sole source of all violence, distracting onlookers from the "true goals" of the Black Lives Matter movement.

Aside from inaccurate renderings of the 2020 uprisings as having both a single point of activation as well as a single cause, the designation of anarchist politics, which opposes capitalism and the state, as an entirely white endeavor was a profoundly ahistorical misattribution that erased Black anarchism. White anarchist politics cannot describe adequately or provide an accurate analytic lens for the dynamics of radical movement-making throughout the long, hot summer of 2020. While the proliferation of anarchist tactics and strategies – such as the black bloc, affinity groups, and mutual aid networks that supported the rebellion at a grassroots level – should not be underestimated, there has been and continues to be a disconnect between traditions of anarchism originating in Europe versus those rooted in Black radical tradition within the United States.

For us, the George Floyd rebellion is another entry into the Black radical tradition. We focus on that moment as our collective memory's most important contemporary example of Black resistance to racial capitalism. At the same time, the George Floyd rebellion can be understood as an essential chapter in anarchist history. Black anarchist politics have made a critical resurgence. Organizing networks, articles, zines, podcasts, and meetings have kept the movement for liberation alive long after the flames of 2020. A renewed interest in Black anarchism has flourished within movement spaces, emerging directly from the rebellion.

Where are the Black anarchists? Where do they fit within this moment? How do their politics relate to resurgent Black radicalism and anarchist politics after the rebellion? Abolitionist politics came to the forefront of the George Floyd rebellion. The similarities in ideological commitments against the state among abolitionists, anarchists, and the Black rebels who rebelled are clear. The uprisings in 2020 will continue to influence politics in the United States and the world.

Within the last fifteen years, mass struggles have grown with the emergence of the Occupy Movement, in the segregated cities like Ferguson, in the battles over Indigenous lands such as Standing Rock, and with the 2020 summer of Black insurrection. The intersections between Black radicalism and the anarchist movement hold an often overlooked dynamism at many flashpoints of movement activity. However, as many of the intersections of Black radicalism and the anarchist movement go back to the legacies of the Black Panther Party (BPP) and the Black Liberation Army (BLA), we do not believe one can understand social movements in the United States at this moment without understanding the relationship between anarchism and the Black radical tradition. These dynamics can no longer be ignored, impacting as they do on Black organizing in the aftermath of the George Floyd rebellion.

Anarchism is a radical tradition that takes its name from the Greek "an," meaning "without," and "-arkos," meaning "rulers and/or hierarchy"; anarchism is critical of the state, capitalism, and all forms of domination. It is a practice defined through horizontal organization, direct action, and mutual aid. The Black radical tradition, on the other hand, is a resistance to racial capitalism that people of African descent practice, as theorized by Cedric Robinson in his seminal text Black Marxism: The Making of the Black Radical Tradition (2000). Robinson understood the Black radical tradition as a separate, if often neglected, front that differs from traditional, European and North American left movements that have opposed capitalism.

We seek to define these two radical traditions, understand their practices historically and clarify their implications for current struggles that move through and beyond racial capitalism. There are clear contradictions between Black radicalism and European anarchism. We argue that European-North American anarchism, despite its purported anti-domination politics, maintains an orientation toward a (white) universal working class that has failed comprehensively to theorize and fully embrace a resistance to racial capitalism. Nevertheless, there is a different group of revolutionary anarchist theorists who share some characteristics and theoretical concepts with

European anarchists but who emerged from the Black radical tradition. These are the Black anarchists, a group deriving their politics from the Black radical tradition. Black anarchism developed due to the need to grapple directly with oppressive hierarchies and authoritarian tendencies within Black radicalism and the politics of anti-domination more broadly.

The methodology used in this project involves a deep reading and critical analysis of key texts within anarchism, Black radicalism, and specifically Black anarchism. Our methodology is especially pertinent given that much of what is widely understood as European anarchist literature is not often engaged critically with its racial politics, and even less so by those who openly situate themselves within a radical Black anarchic milieu. Moreover, black anarchism is not an academic discipline and cannot be approached as such; Black anarchist politics resides within a culture of oral tradition, letters from jailed and/or exiled revolutionaries, and self-published literature in the form of zines, primarily because many initial Black anarchist intellectuals emerged from prison struggles.

Writings about Black anarchism show quite different perspectives. Although the theorizations of former Black Panther Party members have tended to dominate the discourse within leftist political circles, this is beginning to change with the advent of Black anarchist writings from a newer generation of organizers, activists, and impacted peoples with experiences ranging the full spectrum of liberation work. Additionally, some other writers comment on the Black radical tradition and its relationship to classical anarchism. Finally, some of the source materials, while less critical of the relationship between European anarchism and Black radical movements, were used because they are critical of Black anarchists. As we argue, there are different camps within Black anarchism, and all are worthy of serious reflection.

The first part of our argument involves criticism of European-North American anarchist theory, mainly as it has manifested within the United States. European-North American anarchism, often known as classical anarchism, forms a theoretical canon that emerged from working-class struggles in Europe, alongside Marxism. Although there are several variants within that school of thought, we predominantly focus our critiques on classical individualist and social anarchism. We also discuss the post-classical anarchism that developed during the 20th century, referring to these traditions collectively as European-North American because they derive primarily from anarchist theorists, revolutionary figures, and working-class struggles in Europe and later in North America. We maintain that the European-North American anarchist tradition regarding race manifests class reductionism concerning the nature of capitalism, an orientation that downplays racial capitalism as Robinson describes it and histories of Black resistance to it.

Secondly, we map ideological trends at the intersections between Black radicalism and European-North American anarchist theory, as well as subsequent writing that engages with anarchistic ideas while not directly referring to the European anarchist canon itself. For example, Black anarchic radicals in the United States have stretched anarchism to the material conditions that Black people face under coloniality. We employ the term "stretching" in reference to anti-colonial theorist Frantz Fanon's application of the same term in his book, The Wretched of the Earth (1963). Fanon describes a need to "stretch" Marxism to Third World conditions. Similarly, Black anarchism partly involves a stretching of anarchism to the conditions of Black people.

We distinguish two groups chronologically. The first group includes Black anarchists who emerged from Black liberation struggles, revolutionary nationalism, and prison struggles of the mid-20th century. These figures often engaged directly with European-North American anarchist theory while simultaneously developing analyses of capitalism that extended beyond traditional anarchist views. The second group engages with queer theory, Black feminism, prison abolition, critical race theory, and the works of the first group of Black anarchists. This second group is more diverse in its theorization and influences than the first.

As a key focus, we analyze the different ways that Black anarchists theorize Black struggle and resistance while grounding themselves within a distinctive ideological position. Black anarchists commit to Black self-determination, Black struggle as a nexus of learning and activation, and a critique that differs from that of European-North American anarchists and other Black radicals. This critique emphasizes an experiential and material theorization of racial capitalism and racialized features of other oppressive hierarchies.

In this critical analysis of Black anarchist theory, we explain why Black anarchism holds significance within radical social movements and where it locates itself within both anarchist movements and the Black radical tradition. Most texts referenced here emerged from Black anarchists taking part in struggles and studying on the streets, in prisons, and in their homes, usually far from the academy's gaze, gatekeeping, and referencing styles. Yet, as best we can, we guide readers to places that otherwise might prove challenging to find.

Chapter 2
European and North American Anarchism Confronts Black Radicalism

Black anarchism arose in a challenging context. In addition to dangerous struggles that often led to imprisonment, Black anarchists drew inspiration from the Black radical tradition. Years later, Cedric Robinson clarified the critical elements of this tradition. Robinson's contributions have profoundly influenced the work of more recent Black anarchists.

Elements of European-North American anarchism affected Black anarchists in contradictory and largely negative ways. Helpful features did contribute to some Black anarchist thought and political strategies, for instance, in opposing hierarchical decision-making and resisting the oppressions inherent in the capitalist state. But from the standpoint of the Black anarchists, European and North American anarchism failed to recognize the importance of the Black radical tradition and especially did not reckon adequately with structural racism as an inherent characteristic of racial capitalism ad the capitalist state.

This context manifests in how we organize our writing here. First, this chapter explains the key elements of the Black radical tradition, as clarified by Cedric Robinson's work, that have provided positive inspiration for Black anarchism. Then we describe the characteristics of European-North American anarchism that Black anarchists have opposed for failing to emphasize the importance of structural racism and racial capitalism. Later chapters explain the pathbreaking work of leaders in two waves of Black anarchism that followed the confrontation of European and North American anarchism with Black radicalism.

CEDRIC ROBINSON AND
THE BLACK RADICAL TRADITION

Cedric Robinson's *Black Marxism: The Making of the Black Radical Tradition* analyzes racial capitalism, describes the Black radical tradition and clarifies the relationship between Black radicalism and Marxism. He emphasizes two programs for revolutionary change: Marxism and the Black radical tradition. Robinson argues that Marxism remains a western European ideology despite the emergence of Marxist-inspired movements in non-western areas. Robinson's point is that western cultural and historical experience has informed the "science" of Marxism. Fundamentally, racism

CEDRIC ROBINSON

has permeated the history of capitalism while not receiving a careful analysis in Marxist theory.

Robinson focuses first on the development of racial ideology in western civilization and the subsequent consequences. Here he describes the emergence of racial capitalism. Specifically, he analyzes the formation of Europe partially through colonialism by northern peoples of the continent against the "barbarians" in the Mediterranean region to the south. This analysis emphasizes how slave labor was the basis of production that would continue into the 20th century. He describes the appearance of Europe's first bourgeois class, who were mainly traders. Their most precious cargos were slaves. Robinson describes slavery as the savior of the bourgeoisie. He argues, "European civilization is not the product of capitalism. On the contrary, the character of capitalism can only be understood in the social and historical appearance [of slavery]" (Robinson, 2000:24). He also describes how Europeans tended to exaggerate regional differences and interpret them as racial differences. According to Robinson, this racialization affected the Slavs in the earlier Middle Ages and the Tartars in Italian cities later. Finally, people in what Robinson calls the Third World came to fill the category of "slave." Europe was never a free and equal society, as racialization and racism permeated material reality.

In the second part of Robinson's study, he focuses on the other Black radical tradition that is not Marxism. He describes how this tradition emerged as a response to racial capitalism because the urban proletariat did not solely constitute the revolutionary subject. Robinson details how the exploitation of

Black labor power through slavery was essential for the development of modern capitalism. Thus, the revolutionary subject could not just be a factory worker.

Robinson describes some of the resistance in the African diaspora and the continent that he categorizes within the Black radical tradition. He suggests that Marx did not anticipate "the embryo of a demon that would be visited on the whole enterprise of primitive accumulation" (Robinson 122). Effectively, Robinson argues that Marxist accounts of history do not recognize that slave cargos were not just slaves. These laborers had cultures that translated into resistance: "These cargoes, then, did not consist of intellectual isolates or deculturated Blacks – men, women, and children separated from their previous universe. African labor brought the past with it, a past that had produced it and settled on it the first elements of consciousness and comprehension" (Robinson, 2000:121-122). Enslaved people were not just passive. Instead, Robinson argues that the idea of the passive slave is historically inaccurate.

Slavery emerged from the slave regime's brutality and slave resistance in the forms of sabotage, assassination, stealing, escape, and insurrection. Slavery could not alter the being of captive Africans, and they never completely became slaves. He goes on to describe slave resistance historically. Some historical examples include maroonage, referring to slaves' escape from slavery, as well as the founding of palenques, mocambos, and quilombos in North and South America. These settlements of escaped slaves were autonomous, often rebellious, settlements striking back at the slave system. He describes resistance in numerous locales, highlighting revolutionary slave actions in colonial North America, including the establishment of maroon colonies in Florida and the Carolinas and the slave resistance during the U.S. War for independence. Later, he describes the Haitian Revolution and the contribution of maroon colonies to that struggle. The captive African never became wholly the slave, according to Robinson.

Robinson also traces the ideological, philosophical, and epistemological nature of Black revolutionary movements. He describes how a lack of "mass violence predominantly defined the movement against slavery." Black resistance never showed the same degree of violence that white settlers had utilized. The revolutionary violence in the Black radical tradition flowed from impulse rather than a more extensive understanding of violence. The Black radical tradition draws deeply on the idea of the masses' impulse to make history on "their own terms." The resistance that responded to slavery and imperialism casts doubts on the idea that capitalism can remake human experience to strip away all vestiges of culture.

Before writing Black Marxism, Robinson engaged with anarchism in his work about political authority. The fifth chapter of his work, The Terms of Order (2016), deals specifically with European anarchism in contrast with anarchism in African societies. He argues that "anarchism developed as a specific negation to the evolution of a political authority – the State – which served to orchestrate and to some degree mystify the structure of economic relations.... To put it in a general way, we will be contrasting an anarchism rooted in a politically ordered society to an anarchism rooted in a traditionally nonpolitical community."

Although he wrote The Terms of Order before Black Marxism, Robinson was already engaging the Black radical tradition in the sense that kinship as an ordering principle had become a component for Black radical movements resistant to racial capitalism. He does not situate the African "anarchist" societies as a response to racial capitalism. His criticism of anarchism comes from the idea that the anarchism of the West is a negation of Western political authority. At the same time, the Black radical tradition repudiates all the West or, in the case of African anarchism, it simply exists separate from the West: "They [anarchists of the West] had failed to free themselves, to disengage meaningfully from the existential boundaries and force of their own experience. They were (and are) forever in the state clawing out to a thing perceived through the eyes of naive, desperate infancy" (Robinson, 2016:185). His claim here is that the European anarchists could not move beyond the authority of the western state, despite their desire to move to something outside the state. Western anarchism is a political position of opposition to the European state. Some of the works by Black anarchists that we will discuss later echo these ideas.

WHERE EUROPEAN AND NORTH AMERICAN ANARCHISM GOES WRONG ABOUT RACE

To start, we mention some counter-evidence to our argument that European and North American anarchism have not addressed key elements of Black radicalism. In addition to Black anarchist writers and activists who see a tension between the Black radical tradition and anarchism (whom we describe in the next chapter), many leftist anarchist writers share similar critiques about the nature of anarchist organizing.

Paramount among these works is the piece Between Infoshops and Insurrection by Joel Olson, as it articulates the most explicit critique of anarchist organizing. In this work, Olson criticizes the anarchist movement for several reasons concerning Black struggle. Olson makes four main points in his paper: He argues that "[c]ritiques of power that conflate all structures and oppression as equal on moral grounds lack an understanding of how particular structures and oppressions shape and function in each society" (Olson, 2009). His critique comes from the position that anarchists, while opposing all oppression, do not understand how the United States was built around slavery and that they need to focus on combating racism as a strategy for revolutionary anarchism:

> The critique of hierarchy, in other words, confuses a moral condemnation of all forms of oppression with a political and strategic analysis of how power functions in the United States. It resists the notion that in certain historical contexts, certain forms of hierarchy play a more central role in shaping society than do others. It assumes

that because all forms of oppression are evil and interconnected that fighting any form of oppression will have the same revolutionary impact (Olson, 2009).

Olson then relates this argument to DuBois' statement that "the primary reason for the failure of the development of a significant anti-capitalist movement in the United States is white supremacy" (Olson, 2009).

Finally, Olson describes how the anarchist movement in the United States is essentially a subculture with little desire to build a movement. This leads him into his final critique of the lifestylism of the anarchist movement that "... has led it to ignore the most important and radical political tradition in the United States: the Black freedom movements against slavery, segregation, and other forms of racial oppression" (Olson, 2009). Fundamentally, he makes the argument that the anarchist movement ignores the Black radical tradition. He describes how certain figures within the Black radical tradition had anarchistic elements in their organizing. Olson mentions William Lloyd Garrison, the South Carolina Commune, and Ella Baker's anti-authoritarian critique of Martin Luther King. Olson notes Lorenzo Ervin and Kuwasi Balagoon, whom we discuss later, as well as the Black Autonomy Federation, Love and Rage, and Anarchist People of Color as examples of groups attempting to link the Black radical tradition with anarchism.

George Ciccariello-Maher's piece, "An Anarchism That is Not Anarchism: Notes toward a Critique of Anarchist Imperialism" (2011), continues the direction of Olson's work. Ciccariello-Maher begins by discussing how Black Flame, a recent anarchist text that attempts to revive the syndicalist and classical traditions, attempts to situate anarchism as a part of the Enlightenment Period. By placing it as a part of the Enlightenment, the Black Flame analysis situates anarchism within a Eurocentric model:

> Hence we already see that the two sides of our critique are utterly inseparable and that between European Enlightenment rationality and the project of racialization and colonization there exists a relationship of fundamental complicity, as with two sides of a single sordid coin (Ciccariello-Maher, 2011:21).

Ciccariello-Maher's reference to classical anarchism as a product of the Enlightenment, which in turn was associated with racialization and colonialism, relates to Cedric Robinson's theory of racial capitalism and other anti-colonial anarchist critiques of European anarchism. Fundamentally, classical anarchism emerged from European racialized rationality. Eurocentric anarchism does not deal adequately with the materialities of racism and revolutionary politics. Continuing the work of Joel Olson, where he criticizes the anarchist movements in the early 2000s, Ciccariello-Maher understands how this division between anarchist theory and racial realities exists materially in organizing spaces as well. Seeing anarchism as a product of European ideology is critical to grasping why anarchists have not prioritized fighting racism and building relationships with Black communities.

Aside from occasional critiques of anarchism from within the anarchist movement, the character of European-North American anarchism as manifested within North America reveals a class reductionism concerning race and class. Through this analysis, European anarchists often downplay the role of Black resistance movements to racial capitalism, as well as the capacity of Black communities to act in an anarchistic way. Therefore, we will collectively refer to these anarchism(s) as European-North American because we believe they enact an ideological commitment to a European-North American and / or a uniquely white project.

The class-reductionist anarchists have focused little on the United States as a racialized society. Nor indeed have they focused on capitalism as a racialized political-economic system. We are not saying that anarchists do not oppose racism. However, from the classical period to the contemporary times, we believe that anarchists have inadequately attempted to develop a substantial theory about racism that situates it as central to the development and maintenance of capitalism. They have not, we believe, implemented an anti-racist revolutionary practice based on such a theory. We examine the actions anarchists took and the ideas and ideologies they adopted concerning race and capitalism.

Anarchism differs substantially from Marxism concerning race and racial capitalism. As David Graeber discusses, anarchism has always been about political practice and direct action. We will discuss this viewpoint by looking at four historical periods and modes of thought within anarchism and show how:

1. The individualist anarchist strain of thought became influential in the early 19th century;

2. Anarcho-communism of the late 19th century fell into a "workerist" and class reductionist line.

3. Anarcho-pacifism and subcultural anarchism arose during the 1960s and engaged with the Black liberation movements.

4. Contemporary anarchism (post-1980) adopted new analytical frameworks while continuing to have trouble with the analysis of racial domination.

European-North American anarchism has manifested the second and third of these primary tendencies, especially regarding the Black radical tradition and the oppression of Black communities. Both movements lack an adequate analysis of race and class or racial capitalism. The workerist / economistic tendency has remained in many strains of U.S. anarchism. U.S. anarchism has shown a subcultural tendency, partly due to an emphasis on prefigurative politics. The focus on prefiguring the world tends to exclude people who are not already living according to the favored image of future society.

1. Individualist anarchism

There is a long history of individualist anarchism within the U.S. anarchist tradition. They were mostly subcultural and unconcerned with pursuing a political struggle to liberate Black people. Individualist anarchists tended to oppose slavery, and some were linked to abolitionists. Lewis Perry, in Radical Abolitionism, states that "European anarchism defined itself by attacking slavery" (Perry, 1996:310). But European thinkers used the term slavery loosely rather than as a description for chattel slavery. For instance, Perry describes how the European anarchist Pierre-Joseph Proudhon identified slavery as the "complete invasion, or theft of the life of another" (Perry, p.24). Proudhon and many other European anarchists expanded the definition of slavery to include their exploitation by the capitalist ruling class. But this conception became the limit of European anarchism, as it misunderstood the system of chattel slavery in which enslaved people were considered not human but property, like cattle, whose descendants were to remain chattel slaves. None of the anti-slavery activists of the period, such as Frederick Douglass, identified themselves as anarchists. The inability of European-North American anarchism to develop a concrete material analysis of slavery and racial domination is a problem that continues even now (Perry, p.32-33).

Benjamin Tucker was the principal anarchist of the early individualist U.S. period from the 1830s to 1880s. Tucker fundamentally differed from later anarcho-communists in that his anarchism came from the U.S. as opposed to European tradition. Shone discusses several influences on Tucker and other early anarchists of the United States, including the Declaration of Independence, Jeffersonian democracy, radical Protestantism, and Emersonian individualism (Shone, 2010:16). He asserts that the U.S. anarchist tradition did not emerge from class struggle, as did anarchism in Europe.

Furthermore, we argue that embracing U.S. ideals reveals a lack of an understanding about the nature of racial capitalism. Tucker was a proud patriot even as he admired European individualist anarchists like Proudhon and Max Stirner, who actively rejected nationalism (Shone, 2010:18). At the same time, many individualist anarchists opposed slavery staunchly, although they did not do it on a militant or proactive basis. Tucker defined his ideology as "philosophical anarchism," which rejected the need for political struggle inherent in forms of anarchism such as mutualism or anarcho-communism (Shone, 20). Philosophical anarchism, Tucker argued, employed argument and discussion to bring about an anarchist society. With a lack of class struggle analysis concerning race, the individualist anarchists avoided a commitment to building a movement to abolish the state. This trait continues in the subcultural tendency of some anarchist or anarchist-leaning groups that attempt to create utopian communities outside the state instead of engaging in struggles to move beyond the capitalist state.

The actions of anarchists in the United States have failed to confront racial capitalism partially due to theoretical histories discouraging class and movement struggle. Cedric Robinson defined the history of enslaved Africans as a "Black radical tradition" that took on racial capitalism. However, as Tucker described it, "The Anarchists are simply Unterrified Jeffersonian Democrats" (Shone, 2010:21). This statement alone illustrates how anarchists in the early individualist period actively embraced a political philosophy that justified the enslavement of stolen African peoples. Jefferson was a slave owner, and his liberalism was rooted in the colonial understanding of the primary relational positionality of the period, that of a master to his slaves. Tucker was vehemently anti-socialist in many ways and defined all strains of anarcho-communism, communism, and socialism as "state-socialism" (Shone, 2010:22).

In political thought, Tucker separated anarchism from the slave abolitionist movement.

> Now, we anarchists are political abolitionists. We earnestly desire the abolition of the state. Our position on this question is parallel in most respects to those of the Church abolitionists and the slavery abolitionists (Tucker, quoted in Shone 2013).

Tucker did not view the abolition of the state as a way to end slavery. He did not see the goals of the slave abolitionists as akin to those of the anarchist position, though he clearly saw a connection in the idea of abolition. Tucker himself never participated in any sort of political action against the slave republic. Similarly, anarcho-communists from Europe were much more in tune with class struggle and continued to enact a politics committed to European projects of anarchism.

2. Anarcho-communist and anarcho-syndicalist movements

This second major strand of anarchism began in the mid to late 19th century and stretched into the early 20th century (1870s-1930s). For many, this period is considered the golden age of U.S. anarchism. George Woodcock identifies an "immigrant anarchism" (1962:460) that was introduced to the United States during mass migrations from Europe in the late 19th century. Many European immigrant anarchists were not white in the historical sense of the word. Woodcock distinguishes it from the individualist anarchism that was much more closely linked to the U.S. nativist identity rather than European sources. Different from the individualist anarchists in both form and function, the revolutionary anarchists advocated for violence and the overthrow of the ruling class.

Anarcho-communists of the late 19th century were still informed by the European anarchist emphasis on class without an analytic surrounding race. In David Roediger's book *Seizing Freedom* (2016), he discusses how anarchists Lucy and Albert Parsons were influenced by "Jubilee," referring to the cyclical moment of liberation, abolition, and emancipation after the Civil War. He describes how the Parsons found their place during the struggle for freedom in Texas during Reconstruction (2016:203). Lucy Parsons, who identified alternately as Indigenous, Mexican, and Black, was believed by many to have been a formerly enslaved person freed from a plantation. And though the couple considered themselves to be radical Republicans, Albert Parsons eventually left the Republican Party for the Marxist International Workingman's Association and found himself propelled into radical politics during the Chicago Strike of 1877 (Roediger, 2016:204).

However, Roediger describes how the anarchist movement, epitomized by Parsons, failed to respond to the Black freedom struggle. Similar to individualist anarchists, the anarchists of this period, according to Roediger, made overtures for the rights of Black people while remaining in a class reductionist perspective overall. Lucy Parsons attributed the racial violence of the period to class interests in a typical class reductionist and Marxist sense. According to Shone, "Lucy often characterized racial problems through a Marxist lens, stressing class rather than race as an explanation for ethnic conflicts and exploitation" (Shone, 2010:70). Shone cites various scholars, including Robin D.G. Kelley, who describes her as operating within the confines of white socialist thought. Roediger also touches on her relationship to race; he recounts how Lucy said that "outrages" were heaped upon on the "negro," not because he was Black, but rather because "[...]he is poor. It is because he is dependent." Lucy Parsons chose actively not to identify as Black but rather as Mexican and other backgrounds.

Roediger also describes how Albert Parsons's analysis of race failed in part due to his frequent comparison between chattel slavery and wage slavery (2016:205-206). According to Roediger, Albert agreed with Jefferson Davis that wage slavery was a more effective way to exploit Black workers. Though it is clear that the Parsons were both committed to projects that were anti-racist, the anti-racism they espoused came second to their class politics. There was no acknowledgment of the Black struggle as important as or relevant within – let alone primary to – the organized labor struggle.

Similarly, Emma Goldman's racial politics resembled the precedent set by the Parsons. Goldman acknowledged the existence of racial violence and, in fact, decried it, according to Kathy Ferguson in her book Emma Goldman: *Political Thinking in the Streets*. Ferguson notes that "Race is not absent from Goldman's political thinking; it is present yet in a way that obscures rather than clarifies racial power" (Ferguson, 2013). This distinction in obscuring racial power brings us back to the main thrust of our argument about anarchism: While we are not saying that anarchists have ever ignored racial problems in the United States, we do make the argument that anarchists in the United States have not struggled for Black liberation in a manner that makes it as central to political struggle as class struggle.

Ferguson goes on to describe this phenomenon within Goldman's thinking by showing how a statement by Goldman about the plight of the

Negro illuminated nine different important points about Goldman's thoughts about the relationships between race and class. We are going to discuss the last three points below.

1. The situation is "sad and deplorable," adjectives suggesting sympathy more than struggle.

2. The problem is defined as the negro question, rather than, say, the white question or the slavery question.

3. No struggle against racism is recognized; no Black writers or activists are named as political actors contesting race relations (Ferguson 2013).

Goldman's characterizing the situation in sympathetic tones seems to place her within a similar position to Lucy Parsons in describing "the Negro situation" as "outrageous." Goldman did not fundamentally see the violence of whites against Blacks as a part of a larger struggle against racial capitalism. The eighth point defining it as a *Negro* question shows that Goldman was not anticipating any analysis of whiteness as a concept.

A chasm separating Goldman from Black writers and activists exists because of this situation. Goldman did not envision herself as aligned with any sort of Black liberation struggle, which was in keeping with the anarchism of the Parsons. Moreover, Ferguson describes Goldman's belief that "while white workers need to change their attitudes toward blacks, Black workers need to learn to fight in the first place." Goldman praised John Brown for his militant struggle against slavery – his was the sort of politics she recognized as radical – but, as Ferguson shows, "she gave no credence to struggles for legal reform, no matter what their context" (Ferguson, 2013).

The idea that "Black workers need to learn to fight" erases centuries of resistance across the Black diaspora. Her suggestion that Black folks were somehow helpless and were not fighting in the first place shows either a direct misunderstanding of history or a belief in Black docility, which shows the conflict between the European anarchist perception of political actors and the living Black radical tradition. The idea that Goldman praised Brown as radical for his militant struggle against slavery while suggesting that Black workers needed to learn how to fight illustrates a lack of appreciation for the Black radicalism that consistently had attacked the racial capitalist order about which Robinson writes.

Ferguson later explains how Goldman described Black prisoners as "simple and childlike and trusting." This language, Ferguson argues, she used "to talk about any people, including Ernest Hemingway, Bertrand Russell, and the Russian and Irish peasantry, who she felt were good of heart but lacked an adequate political analysis" (Ferguson 2013). Clearly, Goldman had little understanding about the Black movement's struggle against racial capitalism and seemed to dismiss or not recognize the active role of Black resistance to slavery and capital.

In *Seizing Freedom*, Roediger analyzes the tragedy of missed connections during that period. Frederick Douglass's rise to prominence as an abolitionist illustrates the missed solidarities that would become ingrained in U.S. anarchism during the years to come. Douglass remained silent on the Haymarket Martyrs, according to Roediger, while remarking that "Anarchists do not have a monopoly on bomb-making, and the Negro will soon learn" (Roediger, 2016:208). The disconnect between the anarchist movement and Black radical tradition becomes clear in Douglass's affirmation that anarchists of the immigrant working class were not the only people living under the boot of U.S. capitalism and his understanding that violence became a viable tool against oppression. The Boston Republican, an abolitionist newspaper that was sympathetic to violence in service to liberation of Black people, frequently derided the anarchist violence in Chicago as "having no cause" (Roediger, 2016:208).

3. Anarcho-pacifism and subcultural anarchisms

The third major historical strand of anarchism in the United States is that described in Andy Cornell's book *Unruly Equality* (2016), where the author examines the interactions between anarchists and the civil rights movement. We would locate this period from roughly 1930 to 1985. Cornell argues that anarchists began turning to the examples set by Black freedom movements due to failed efforts to organize labor. He focuses on four flash points of the civil rights movement: the Montgomery Bus Boycott, the integrationist efforts in Little Rock, the self-defense movement, and the emergence of the Student Nonviolent Coordinating Committee (SNCC). For each flash point, Cornell tries to clarify how anarchists responded. Additionally, Cornell discusses the interactions between later Black revolutionary nationalism and anarchism.

Cornell's work emphasizes that, although anarchists did engage with oppression of Black people and racism broadly, anarchism of the 1960s lacked an analytic framework to deal with race and class. Anarchists usually did not materially aid the Black revolutionary movements that were opposing the same capitalist powers that the anarchists considered themselves fighting against.

Cornell walks readers through interactions between anarchists and early civil rights leaders. For instance, when he speaks of the Montgomery Bus Boycott. Cornell describes the influence of anarcho-pacifists such as David Dellinger on the non-violence practiced throughout great swaths of the civil rights movement. He also discusses how Bayard Rustin, who had explicit interactions with anarchists though not an anarchist himself, was instrumental in creating the campaign in Montgomery with King (Cornell, 2016:220-221). Support for Rustin's training in non-violence came from the anarchist milieu in the War Resisters League.

Although anarchist non-violent, direct-action practice entered the civil rights movement, no anarchist intervention addressed the question of race and class. Cornell acknowledges this gap, as the civil rights movement combined a variety of traditions including liberalism, Black nationalism, and prophetic radical theology:

> There anarchist tenets such as the equal liberty of all people, the importance and validity of individual resistance to social evil, and direct action by the oppressed became mixed with the social justice traditions of liberalism, the African American church, Black nationalism, and the below-the-radar contributions of communist activists (Cornell, 2016:222).

No anarchists actively participated in the civil rights movement as a part of their revolutionary practice. Regarding anarchists' difficulties in developing a theory of race and class, Cornell points to statements published by an anarchist journal about the need for white workers to unite with Black workers in a union to combat segregation; these statements managed to produce not a single analysis on race.

> Statements such as this indicate that in 1957 the league held to an economistic perspective, which saw class relations as determinant of inequality and social conflict as a whole. From this angle, capitalist exploitation was the true form of injustice, and white working people in Arkansas had been tricked by the ruling class into expressing racism against workers of color" (Cornell, 2016:223).

The economistic view, a lack of intentionally constructed relationships with Black radicals, and advocacy for militant unionism as a solution for the crisis of racism in Arkansas, makes it clear that the class reductionist anarchist position had not changed in a major way since the 19th century, no matter the anarchist engagement in the civil rights movement.

We did not find that the perspective of European or North American anarchists moved beyond an economistic perspective, nor did we see a theory and practice that opposed racial capitalism. Instead, anarchists seemed to deepen their own involvement in subcultural movements located even further away from Black radical movements. Undoubtedly, the anarchists of this period understood that there was a "shameful tradition of discrimination within the U.S. labor movement" (Cornell, 2016:230), and that the economistic politics of anarchism were beginning to break down:

> Dolgoff and other anarchists had long held that conservative union policies stemmed from the misleadership of officials compromised by their positions of power. In contrast, they believed rank-and-file workers would instinctually fight to overturn inequality if their energies were not diverted. Yet they also admitted that workers were themselves at least partly responsible for divisive racism within the unions (Cornell, 2016:231).

Anarchists did not develop a theory and practice to oppose racism from within the labor movement or even a push to understand why racism was happening.

Cornell later describes the anarchist-influenced organizations such as Black Mask and the White Panther Party as having explicit politics connected to Black liberation. These organizations, rather than participating in active movement building and theorizing around how to dismantle racial capitalism, were engaging in many of the subcultural and prefigurative politics that led to the contemporary anarchist movement that began in the 1980s and onwards. For instance, the White Panther Party defined itself by adopting "a ten-point program whose first point was an endorsement of the Black Panther Party's own program. The next nine points, however, built upon the 'Digger concept of 'the Free'" (Cornell, 2016:263) and articulated their politics as a

> ... cultural revolution through a total assault on the culture. . . . we are LSD-driven total maniacs in the universe. We will do anything we can to drive people out of their heads into their bodies. Rock & roll music is the spearhead of our attack because it's so effective and so much fun (Cornell, 2016:264).

Their politics avoided any action in support of Black revolutionary movements and no substantive plan to attack racial capitalism despite their endorsement of the Black Panther Party Platform.

4. Contemporary anarchism

This strand began to emerge in the 1970s through the 1980s and has continued into today. It owes much to prior anarchist orientations, both the individualist and the anarcho-communist cohorts. Contemporary anarchism suffers from many of the same problems that have plagued anarchism historically about acknowledging Black liberation struggles.

Contemporary anarchism has departed from the class-oriented traditions of the late 19th and early 20th centuries while in some ways reengaging with a previous individualist tradition. We agree with Cornell that the shift from classical anarchism to contemporary anarchism occurred primarily because anarchists were engaging with a larger critique of domination through their engagement with the civil rights movement, anti-war activism, and feminism (Cornell, 2016:281-282). But we hold that anarchists developed neither an anti-colonial lens nor any sort of analytic to account for racial domination.

To illustrate this, we focus on anarchist scholars such as David Graeber and the Black Flame Reader as examples of how different strains of contemporary anarchism have attempted to account for racial capitalism while failing to deal fully with its dynamics. According to Graeber, the United States was a nation built on white supremacy and whiteness was a category of privilege: The only way to destroy a system of privilege that vast and ingrained was to be a race traitor (Graeber, 2010:241). However, Graeber then goes on to suggest that being a race traitor is difficult if you have anarchist politics because "most revolutionary groups in communities of color were far more hierarchically organized – where, in fact, many saw emphases on direct democracy as itself a form of white privilege" (Graeber, 2010:242).

According to Graeber when discussing the formation of the Anarchist People of Color network, people coded as "non-white" were more likely to face police repression (Graeber, 243). While acknowledging the existence of a formation that was not white, Graeber suggests that direct action was viewed by many "POC activist groups" as privileged (Graeber, 2010:243). Graeber implies that anarchist tactics and organizational methods were incompatible with Black or non-white peoples' movements. There is no acknowledgment of the long history of Black resistance and organizing that Robinson describes in his works about the Black radical tradition.

The Black Flame Reader, published in 2009, dismisses everything having to do with the racial nature of capitalism. In fact, *The Black Flame Reader* seems to articulate a class reductionist position similar to the positions of the earlier anarcho-communists. For instance, in the last chapter, the authors articulate: "For the anarchists and syndicalists, racial divisions undermined popular unity and prevented internationalism, the preconditions for fundamental social change" (Van Der Walt and Schmidt, 2009:299). This approach rejects the idea that "racial divisions" were essential for the development of capitalism. But *The Black Flame Reader* goes further than the anarcho-communists of the 19th century, as it actively rejects the "white privilege thesis." It begins by describing how anarchist lines of thought differ

> ...fundamentally from the analysis of race championed by nationalists, who claim that different races and nationalities have fundamentally incompatible interests. It also differs from modern "identity politics," which envisage society as fragmented "into innumerable and irreconcilable strata with different "privileges" according to class, gender, nationality, sexual orientation, and race (Van Der Walt and Schmidt, 2009:303).

To reject an analysis of white privilege as coming from an "analysis of race" championed by nationalists, rather than as a meaningful analysis about the material consequences of racialized capitalism, is emblematic of how the anarchist movement has struggled with developing an analysis of racial capitalism.

Black Flame makes a similar argument to Graeber and Cornell about how politics focused around a racial analysis have a tendency to become authoritarian (Van Der Walt and Schmidt, 2009:303). Such a recurrent tendency of anarchist authors to label critiques of whiteness and analytical tools around race as authoritarian is disturbing to us. It is partly why, in the second part of this work, we trace the anarchist roots of movements within the Black radical tradition.

Chapter 3
The Evolution of
Black Anarchist Politics

BLACK ANARCHISM: WHAT IS IT?

Due to the lack of explicitly Black anarchist formations and the presence of disparate people theorizing about it, Black anarchism is not clearly defined ideologically. Black anarchism is not simply Black people engaging with the European-North American anarchist canon uncritically and doing usual "anarchist" things while happening to be Black. Instead, we argue that Black anarchism has a theoretical trajectory that is separate from prior anarchist traditions, although some Black anarchist theorists have drawn from these earlier traditions.

Black anarchism centers on historical and contemporary struggles for Black self-determination and against white supremacy, but it also encompasses other issues. Some versions of Black anarchism are more class-oriented, while others emphasize destroying all hierarchy or domination. The Black radical tradition provides a key basis for Black anarchism, which owes more to Malcolm X, the Black Panther Party, the Maroons, and African influences than to European or North American non-Black anarchist thinkers. While Black anarchism emerged mainly from the Black radical tradition, as analyzed by Cedric Robinson in Black Marxism, few Black anarchists reference Robinson directly. While not emerging from European-North American anarchism, Black anarchism applies some concepts from these earlier traditions to the Black context, such as mutual aid, struggle against all forms of domination, autonomy, and direct action. In this part of our work, our goal is to clarify the influences of Black radical thought on the development of Black anarchism to understand how various orientations of Black anarchists theorize race and emphasize political action.

TWO WAVES OF BLACK ANARCHISM

We are focusing on the history and manifestations of Black anarchism, mainly in the United States. Therefore, we do not engage the work of African anarchists such as Sam Mbah (Mbah and Igariwey, 1997) and the history of anarchistic societies on the African continent. However, because some texts concerning African history did influence Black anarchism in the United States, we mention those. One focus is the interaction between Black radicalism in the United States and European-North American anarchist theory, which has resulted in various strands of Black anarchism. To understand Black anarchism, it is vital to see its emergence not among Black adherents of European-North American anarchist theory but among Black radicals modifying limited components of anarchism for their use in Black liberation.

As we mentioned, there is no single type of Black anarchist politics. Black anarchist thought comes in several different forms. We organize them into two historical waves and define the two waves primarily by their ideological character and place historically. Although we give historical dates, the boundaries are fluid, as many first-wave anarchists continue to organize and interact with the second-wave anarchists. We use the term "wave" as the ideological trends are not uniform but share a general direction. We trace the first wave to the Black radical movements of the mid-20th century, while the second wave is developing in our current moment.

The first wave, which we place between 1965 and 2000, includes the figures who initially applied anarchist ideas as participants in the Black liberation struggles of the 1960s and 1970s. Many of these anarchists were members of the Black Panther Party, the Black Liberation Army, or other Black revolutionary organizations. We focus on figures such as Martin Sostre (the first Black anarchist as described by his successors), Lorenzo Kom'boa Ervin, Kuwasi Balagoon, and Ashanti Alston. We do not consider them all as "anarcho-Pantherists" because many of them defined themselves differently as "New Afrikan anarchists" or "Black autonomists.".

A useful way to understand the first wave of Black anarchist thought is to compare how Frantz Fanon discusses the application of Marxism to the colonial world. Fanon argues that Marxism needed to be stretched in the colonial context, where usual versions of Marxism do not work (1963: chapter 1 ("On Violence")). Likewise, we think that much of the Black anarchists' theoretical work in the first wave has stretched anarchism to the colonial conditions in the United States.

To some degree, all Black anarchists in the first wave expressed the idea of internal colonialism within the United States and the inability of U.S. anarchism to deal with that reality. As Fanon describes:

> The originality of the colonial context is that economic reality, inequality, and the immense difference of ways of life never come to mask the human realities.... In the colonies the economic substructure is also a superstructure. The cause is the consequence; you are rich because you are white, you are white because you are rich. This is why Marxist analysis should always be slightly stretched every time we have to do with the colonial problem (Fanon, 1963:40).

Fanon argued that Marxism needed to be stretched to the colonial conditions, and the first wave of Black anarchists committed to a project that stretched anarchist politics to the Black colony in the United States. However, we do not categorize the second wave as a "stretching" of anarchism to the Black colonial condition in the United States because some Black anarchist theoreticians do not explicitly name the Black condition in the United States as a colonial relationship. Also, while the first wave clearly distinguishes between their Black anarchism and European-North American anarchism, the second wave does not.

The second wave of Black anarchists emerged in the 21st century, especially around the struggles against the police and prisons in the post-Ferguson moment. This wave has only deepened and grown since the George Floyd Rebellion, which happened after we began this project. Many participants in the second wave engage directly with the work of the first wave while including new frameworks, especially Black feminism and queer theory. The development of the Anarkata Turn (a Black anarchistic formation) and the work of people like Zoé Samudzi and William C. Anderson (2018) shows the inclusion and importance of Black feminist and queer theory for Black anarchist politics. This orientation sets the second wave apart from the first wave, as the theorizing does not emerge directly from Black revolutionary nationalist organizing circles. *The Anarkata Statement* also emphasizes disability justice and Pan-Africanism, which differentiates it from the work of Samudzi and Anderson.

In general, the second wave draws from various influences and is less attached to the ideas of anarchism so much as the values within it. The second wave also references the first wave of Black anarchists while often broadening the analysis. We place the beginning of the second wave during the mid-1990s, although it starts to establish an ideological presence in the resurgent Black protest movement of the mid-2010s. The second wave has attained wider influence and theoretical clarity during and after the George Floyd Rebellion, with much more of a spotlight on Black anarchist theory from the work of William C Anderson, JoNina Ervin, and Lorenzo Kom'boa Ervin, whose work we address later. The Black Autonomy Podcast has helped draw attention to this work (https://blackautonomy.libsyn.com).

Black anarchism has achieved a theorization of race that, as we showed in our previous chapter, remained largely absent in European-North American anarchist frameworks. In addition, Black anarchist politics also engage with Black nationalism, critique hierarchy, and emphasize some anarchist tactics and practices. This mix can vary widely across the different forms and writers. However, the major distinction remains that Black anarchism is rooted in Black struggle, Black history, and Black radical movements. It is not simply "Black people" doing anarchism. The influence of some European and North American anarchists is not absent from Black anarchist writing. Still, the Black radical tradition is the primary theoretical and practical source for Black anarchists.

Chapter 4
The First Wave of Black Anarchism

**MARTIN SOSTRE:
THE FIRST BLACK AUTONOMIST**

MARTIN SOSTRE

Martin Sostre consistently receives credit as the genesis for Black anarchist thought. Lorenzo Kom'boa Ervin describes his time spent in prison with Martin Sostre as life-changing. He explains how "we became an Anarchist, a jailhouse lawyer, and a prison activist during the 1970s because of Martin Sostre" (Ervin, 2020). Ervin details his relationship with Sostre in prison and how that developed. According to Ervin, Sostre "went through a political metamorphosis from a NOI [Nation of Islam], Black nationalist, and later an Anarchist" (Ervin, 2020). Sostre's transition to anarchist ideology stemmed from his origins within Black radicalism. His move from various forms of Black radicalism into anarchism is a trend frequently occurring in much

Black anarchist writing. Ervin describes his interactions with Sostre in prison:

> The initial ideas for Black autonomy, within the overall Anarchist movement, came from these sessions.... He told me endlessly that Socialism and Anarchism were for all people, not just Europeans and well-to-do intellectuals. It was universal. At first, we had serious doubts about all this, as it seemed just more white radical student ideology. They were not sympathetic to the Black struggle, and they were not working class or poor. Sostre's ideas, however, were that Anarchists of color must build their "wing" of the Anarchist movement. He didn't call it Black Autonomy, but that is what it was (Ervin, 2020).

Ervin's attribution of the idea of Black autonomy to Sostre highlights how Black anarchism is not simply Black people partaking in a European-North American anarchist tradition. Ervin discusses his skepticism about applying anarchist ideas to the Black struggle. Sostre's understanding of the need for a separate wing of the anarchist movement adds weight to the notion that Black anarchism is a political movement and ideology developed from the Black struggle in the streets and prisons. Anarchism, according to Sostre, must be defined by the Black struggle, not by Europeans or non-Black North Americans.

Sostre's incarceration and subsequent campaign for freedom places his anarchism within a prison revolutionary organizing tradition, which has been an essential part of Black anarchism. The development of Black anarchism has always been linked to the prison struggle that we will explain later. Sostre served a sentence in the early 1960s in Attica prison. After serving his sentence, he created the Afro-Asian Bookstore in Buffalo, New York (Ervin, 2020). According to Ervin, "Sostre's bookstore became a center of radical thought and political education in that city. A Black 'riot' against police brutality against a Black youth broke out at this time, and Sostre was blamed for this rebellion since many youths visited his bookstore" (Ervin, 2020). Sostre's subsequent frame-up by the white political establishment after his first time in prison is important to understand in a larger context. His persecution for inciting a riot casts him into the role of the traditional "anarchist." At the same moment, he is different for his advocacy of Black causes rather than just the "class struggle," as someone like Albert Parsons.

PORTRAIT OF MARTIN SOSTRE BY SHANNON FAUWKES

The development of Black anarchism emerges from the Black radical tradition in the form of the prison revolutionary. This role differentiates him from European anarchist traditions, which emerged predominantly from working-class immigrant experiences during the 19th century in the United States. As a Black anarchist, Sostre provides the basis for Lorenzo Ervin's later theorizing of Black autonomy. Sostre serves as an example of a continuing trend within Black anarchist thought.

LORENZO KOM'BOA ERVIN: THEORIST OF BLACK REVOLUTION

Lorenzo Kom'boa Ervin

Lorenzo Kom'boa Ervin's contributions as an anarchist and a Black revolutionary theorist are often overlooked. His seminal work, *Anarchism and the Black Revolution* (1993), and his criticism of the white anarchist milieu in *The Progressive Plantation* (2011) decades later are significant contributions to Black anarchism. These contributions, in our view, provide a basis from which most other Black anarchists derive, especially Black anarchists in the second wave, such as Samudzi, Anderson, and the Anarkatas.

Understanding the personal history of someone like Ervin is key to understanding his politics and theories. In an interview with Libcom.org, Ervin described his involvement with the movement beginning with the 1960 sit-ins and Black rebellions against the police in Chattanooga. Ervin subsequently was involved with SNCC and then the Black Panther Party after the merger between SNCC and the BPP. Ervin came from a Black radical tradition and then engaged with anarchism later in his life as a political prisoner (Ervin and Abron, 2000). Alongside Balagoon, he lays the foundation for the disjuncture between European-North American forms of anarchism and Black radicals. His contributions show the importance of an analysis incorporating racism into an anarchist vision.

Ervin was a revolutionary organizer before he was a theorist. This pattern follows an anarchistic tradition of deed over theory. He came to anarchism through struggle. Ervin's texts, *Anarchism and the Black Revolution* and *The Progressive Plantation*, represent different moments in Ervin's political consciousness. In *Anarchism and the Black Revolution*, he articulates a vision more inspired by syndicalism, while his politics, later on, focus more explicitly on the tension between Black, indigenous, and people of color versus the state in North America. His theorizing lays a foundation for other forms of Black anarchism.

Ervin's theorization of "white skin privilege" is an essential contribution to Black anarchist politics and anarchist politics as a whole that he articulates in *The Progressive Plantation*:

> White skin privilege is a form of domination by Capital over white labour as well as oppressed nationality labour, not just providing material incentives to "buy off" white workers and set them against Black and other oppressed workers. This explains the obedience of white labour to Capitalism and the State. The white working class does not see their better off condition as part of the system of exploitation. After centuries of political and social indoctrination, they feel their privileged position is just and proper, and what is more has been "earned" (Ervin, 2011:7).

Understanding white skin privilege as a form of domination by capital over labor is essential. White skin privilege departs dramatically from the prior anarchist theorizing of race and class or lack thereof. Ervin's theorizing forms the basis of Black anarchism moving forward. In contrast, some Black anarchists in the later wave are less insistent about class struggle as a central dynamic than Ervin is. Ervin engages with questions of race rather than shying away, as many European and North American anarchists do.

This approach translates into his argument about the need for Black autonomy. In his earlier work *Anarchism and the Black Revolution*, his theorizing derives from ideas about class and race, where he describes the "self-activity" of Black workers.

> Because of the dual forms of oppression of non-white workers and the depth of social desperation it creates, Black workers will strike first, whether their potential allies are available to do so or not. This self-determination is why it is necessary for oppressed workers to build independent movements that unite their own peoples first. This self-activity of the oppressed masses (such as the Black Liberation movement) is inherently revolutionary, and is an essential part of the social revolutionary process of the entire working class. This is why it is important for white workers to defend the rights and gains of non-white workers. These are not marginal issues; they cannot be downgraded or ignored by white workers if the goal is revolutionary transformation. This key principle, that oppressed peoples have a right to self-determination, includes the right to run their own organizations and liberation struggles. The victims of racism know best how to fight back against it (Ervin, 1993).

Ervin's rhetoric moves to the language of self-determination under a Black revolutionary tradition. His acknowledgment of "self-activity" can be understood in resonance with some Marxist theories of spontaneity. Black Marxists such as C.L.R. James or Kiamanthi Mohammed wrote explicitly about this phenomenon. Ervin situates the self-activity of the Black masses as central to the class struggle. White anarchists cannot reduce the importance of self-activity among Black communities. The self-activity of the Black working class must not be viewed as marginal but as the "cardinal principle."

To Ervin, the struggle against racism will define whether or not a successful working-class movement will emerge. Struggles for self-determination led by oppressed peoples will define the fight against racism. Understanding that the Black worker is fundamentally a subject with revolutionary capacity is a crucial part of Ervin's argument. He would attribute this revolutionary capacity partly to the dual oppression (race and class) that Black workers face.

In *The Progressive Plantation*, a pamphlet about his experiences in the Occupy movement, Ervin identifies Black people in the United States as colonized people.

> Blacks (or Africans in America) are colonized. America is a mother country with an internal colony, made up of Black people who have been enslaved and oppressed for centuries.... Ours is a captive, oppressed colonial status that must be overthrown, not just smashing ideological racism or denial of civil rights (Ervin, 2011:8).

The idea of the internal colony also arises in the work of Kuwasi Balagoon, who identifies as a New Afrikan anarchist. A similar idea of internal colony goes back to the work *Black Power* written by Kwame Ture and Charles Hamilton in 1966 (Ture and Hamilton, 1967).

Ervin goes on to describe the importance of Black autonomous movements and Black nationalism.

> This requires the Black Liberation movement to liberate themselves from a colonial existence, based on capitalism and this is why it is not just a simple matter of Blacks just joining with white Anarchists to fight the same type of battle against the State. That is also why Anarchists cannot take a rigid position against all forms of Black Nationalism (especially revolutionary groups like the original Black Panther Party, which was both radical and Socialist) even if there are ideological differences about the way some of them are formed and operate (Ervin, 2011:8).

This valuable point differs from a traditional anarcho-communist view in terms of practice. While a conventional anarcho-communist would approach the non-racialized working class as the most critical site of organization, Ervin departs from acting as an "anarchist who happens to be Black" by locating resistance primarily within Black and colonized populations.

Ervin describes how situating oneself outside the traditional anarchist milieu leads to critique from the rest of the anarchist movement, which white people dominate. Ervin describes various organizations such as Roots of Resistance in Vancouver, the Black Autonomy movement, Colors of Resistance, and others that subsequently "died away because of isolation, lack of material aid, lack of political support and ridicule by the general Anarchist movement. This is disgraceful and does not speak well for Anarchism at all" (Ervin, 2011:25). He describes these groups as "isolated and vilified" within the wider movement. Finally, he discusses how the white anarchist movement has to "make it possible for non-white Anarchists to organize in their communities by providing them with technical resources (printing of zines, video and audio cassette production, etc.), organizer training and assisting them with financial resources to get on their feet. Whatever happened to mutual aid or is that just reserved for white radicals" (Ervin, 2011:25)?

This anarchistic emphasis on mutual aid and revolutionary organization puts Ervin in a distinctly organizational and theoretical context. Ervin's political statement is that the Black liberation struggle must take precedence regarding the idea of deracialized class struggle. He also articulates the insular nature of the "white radicals," which goes back to a more extensive critique of the subcultural tendency in anarchist politics.

Finally, we want to emphasize how Ervin situates himself against authoritarianism that he has observed in both the white and Black left, as well as labeling himself as a Black autonomist.

> Black autonomists ultimately reject vanguardism because as the white left [as well as elements of the Black revolutionary movement] has demonstrated, it erodes and eventually destroys the fragile ties that hold together the necessary principled partnerships between groups and individuals that are needed to accomplish the numerous tasks associated with fighting back successfully and building a strong, diverse, and viable revolutionary movement (Ervin, 1993).

The rejection of authoritarian structures is key to Black anarchist thought. Specifically, the anti-authoritarian critique arises primarily from experiences within white and Black authoritarian organizations. The tendency to critique the authoritarianism of the white and Black left is epitomized in the numerous former Panthers, such as Ervin, Balagoon, and Alston. They have engaged in a deep critique of the Black Panther Party. The tendency to critique organizational hierarchy (even informal hierarchies that exist within the white anarchist movement) will continue to manifest within Black anarchist thought. Most of the time, it is directed at authoritarian Black nationalist organizations. Nevertheless, the rejection of Black authoritarian structures is a more significant trend in which Black anarchism emerges as a movement rooted in the Black struggle.

Ervin's thought should be understood as a foundation for Black anarchism and anarchism in general. In both *As Black as Resistance*

(Samudzi and Anderson, 2018) and *Anarkata: A Statement* (Abolitionfuturist, 2019), the second wave of Black anarchists acknowledge Ervin's crucial influence. His theorization of race and class together is critical as it counterposes class reductionist European-North American anarchism to a new theorization of domination. Further, Ervin's critique of white and Black authoritarians helps define where he locates his politics. Ervin ultimately situates himself in the Black radical tradition and the anarchist tradition. Nevertheless, his ideas continue to permeate and further emphasize our point that Black anarchism emerges out of the Black radical tradition and revolutionary organizing. These themes continue in the work and life of Kuwasi Balagoon.

KUWASI BALAGOON:
NEW AFRIKAN ANARCHIST SOLDIER

Kuwasi Balagoon is identified as a New Afrikan anarchist. Similarly, like Sostre and Ervin, he was imprisoned for participating in the Black liberation movement of the 1960s to 1980s. Balagoon's imprisonment resulted from his involvement with the Black underground as repression of the BPP mounted. He is also one of the first queer Black anarchists to become well known, although the memorial after his death did not reveal this fact. Balagoon died as a result of an AIDS-related illness.

Balagoon's queer figure makes his work all the more innovative. Akinyele Umoja details the erasure of Balagoon's queerness by Black nationalist organizations. This erasure reflects tensions between Balagoon's anarchist politics and the more authoritarian and oppressive elements of some Black nationalist groups. Albert "Nuh" Washington reflects upon this in his piece "On Kuwasi Balagoon," which he wrote as a tribute to Balagoon after his death. Washington reflects:

> Because it has been reported that Kuwasi died of AIDS people have a tendency to speculate on how he came by it. In Amerikkka we are told the high-risk groups are homosexuals and intravenous drug users. And for the Black Nationalist, these are no no's. So to make his death acceptable some may theorize the pigs infected him" (Washington, 1986).

Washington comments on how Black nationalists reduced Balagoon's queer identity as they attributed his death from an AIDS-related disease as something that the pigs gave him, as opposed to understanding that Kuwasi's life may not have fit with the values of hetero-patriarchy and stigmatization of drugs that were present in Black nationalist politics.

Balagoon continued to chart his own path as a Black anarchist. Part of Balagoon's legacy emerges from Ashanti Alston's writing about him as a figure within the lumpenproletariat, which also can be connected to his queer politics. Alston describes Balagoon as lumpen and a lawbreaker throughout his piece "On Kuwasi Balagoon." In addition, Alston refers to how Balagoon's politics "...challenged the dominant reality that held humanity in check, and they challenged us\our dominant revolutionary thinking if IT was holding our humanity and movement activities IN CHECK" (Alston, 2001). Balagoon, a queer black anarchist with a lumpen outlook, placed him at odds with many people, even within Black radical movements. His politics challenged the dominant realities of revolutionary thinking. We see this rebellious and constant critique in later strains of Black anarchist politics, especially *The Anarkata Statement*, which (as discussed later) takes up questions of queerness and disability within the movement.

KUWASI BALAGOON

His commitment to revolutionary Black nationalism and his subsequent development into a self-described New Afrikan anarchist comes from the leadership's internal contradictions and authoritarian impulses within the Black Panther Party (Umoja 209-210). Balagoon encountered anarchism through receiving literature from the Anarchist Black Cross Federation. He desired, according to Umoja, "a democratic process that would unleash the revolutionary potential of the masses and not make them prey to new oppressors" (2015:210). Balagoon's anarchism came partially from his reading of European texts and his experience within authoritarian formations of the Black Panther Party.

To differentiate Balagoon from Ervin on the point of nationalism is essential. Balagoon actively embraced a Black nationalist label of "New

Afrikan," associated with the New Afrikan Independence Movement and the Republic of New Afrika (Umoja, 2015:211). The Republic of New Afrika and the New Afrikan Independence Movement were Black nationalist movements that eventually sought to form a nation-state within the historically five Black Belt states of the Deep South. Although repressed, these movements had a large following in prisons. Balagoon situated anti-imperialism and Black self-determination at the root of his anarchist politics. He still supported land and space for Black people's self-determination (the colony thesis) despite not supporting the state seizing politics of Marxist-Leninists and revolutionary nationalists.

This political position that embraced nationalism and anti-imperialist politics while remaining an anarchist created contradictions with his comrades. Balagoon described these issues in one of his letters:

> Although i share a lot of feelings and principles with the nationalist and anti-imperialist movements i am an Anarchist and feel rather isolated ideologically and low for not pushing our politics as much as i should (Balagoon, 2019:187).

It is clear from Balagoon's writing that he primarily worked alongside Black nationalists and anti-imperialists who were emerging predominantly from Marxist-Leninist rather than anarchist frameworks. Yet, despite tensions, Balagoon valued nationalism and anti-imperialism as essential.

Much of his writing from prison focused on building an anarchist organization around New Afrikan and anti-imperialist values similar to Ervin's. For example, in a letter, he wrote:

> If an anti-imperialist anarchist organization establishes itself and calls for an end to imperialism abroad and within the borders of this hemisphere and supports self determination for oppressed nations and supports the working class struggle against the same monopoly capitalists who reap the lion's share of superprofits from the colonies, it will be the only organization with a complete ideology (Balagoon, 2019:191).

Balagoon pointed out a lack of anti-imperialist anarchist organizations in the United States that support self-determination for oppressed nations. When Balagoon described self-determination for oppressed nations, he implicitly referenced New Afrikan nationalism, Chicano nationalism, and indigenous sovereignty movements. As it manifests in the United States, this critique of anarchism echoed Ervin's.

The only anarchist organization with a complete ideology, according to Balagoon, is one that centers on the Black liberation struggle. Balagoon's writing also is similar to Ervin's as it emphasizes political practice. In "Anarchy Can't Fight Alone" (2012), Balagoon envisioned an anarchism that embraces the "will of the masses" and the necessity of situating resistance among colonized people:

> It is beside the point whether Black, Puerto Rican, Native American and Chicano-Mexicano people endorse nationalism as a vehicle for self-determination or agree with anarchism as being the only road to self-determination. As revolutionaries we must support the will of the masses. It is not only racism but compliance with the enemy to stand outside of the social arena and permit America to continue to practice genocide against the third world captive colonies because although they resist, they don't agree with us. If we truly know that Anarchy is the best way of life for all people, we must promote it, defend it and know that the people who are as smart as we are will accept it. To expect people to accept this, while they are being wiped out as a nation without allies ready to put out on the line what they already have on the line is crazy. Anarchy can't fight alone (Balagoon, 2012).

This vision works similarly with the ideas of racism articulated by Lorenzo Ervin. Anarchism as a vehicle for self-determination of the Third World colonies resonates in Balagoon's and Ervin's works, although their language is different. Balagoon refers to how "Anarchy Can't Fight Alone" (2012), which resembles Ervin's claims about the need for anarchists to unite with national liberation movements rather than staying within small organizations. Balagoon also emphasizes that it is racism and compliance to "stand outside of the social arena and permit America to continue to practice genocide." His argument here is similar to how Ervin emphasizes that the larger anarchist movement should not marginalize the Black struggle.

Balagoon locates the significant resistance against capitalism in the United States within colonized populations. He discusses how "The white working class suffers...as well as being organized by the state and ruling class to combat the liberation of Third World colonies" (2019:228). Locating the white working class as complicit in the oppression of the Black working class and other people within the "Third World colonies," Balagoon's articulation of class politics is distinct from anarchist class reductionist ideology.

Balagoon differs from Ervin partly due to his involvement with the Black underground, which influences much of his writing, especially on the nature of the revolutionary collective as opposed to the Black Commune. For example, at the end of his opening statement during the Brinks trial in 1983, Balagoon emphasizes self-critique and critique of hierarchical structures within the Black underground movement.

> i have thrown our lot in with the revolution and only regret that due to personal shortcomings on our part, failure to accept collective responsibility, and bureaucratic, hierarchical tendencies within the B.L.A. [Black Liberation Army], i haven't been able to contribute as much as i should or build a better defense against our capture due to denial of fuse. i am confident that our comrades still at large will correct their thinking and practice through criticism/self-criticism

and begin to strike consistent blows at the U.S. Imperialist (Balagoon, 1983).

This statement illustrates Balagoon's anarchism in his practice as a guerrilla fighter. He points to his own personal failures to seek more democratic structures within his organization. This self-criticism relates back to the prior point about Black anarchism being closely linked with the critique of hierarchy within Black revolutionary formations and driven by practice.

Balagoon goes on to make explicit critiques of the Black Panther Party's survival programs in one of his letters:

> The idea of collectives was alien to the Black Panther Party. We had different survival programs, and people were involved to be part of them, to donate time, afford to get things/stuff [from] businesses operating inside the community, to use the space of institutions such as churches. But the party, being a hierarchy, could not simply initiate alternatives - it felt it had to lead them - it was to be, in its mind and words, not just the leading party but the sole representative of the Black colony. So there was not any organized effort to take space in the colony and to actually produce (only to distribute) or to provide transport or a militia. It was miles away from all of the a, because it was a hierarchy. To fully take on the power structure in a given area, you got to not only provide alternatives but institutions that render the old ones useless (Balagoon, 2019:188).

Balagoon describes how the collective as an organizational form was foreign to the Black Panther Party. The idea of a collective initiating alternative economic structures that the Party did not directly control is important. Balagoon's politics were located in a critique of hierarchy and vanguardism. His discussion of collectives as a form of organization in his letters collected in A Soldier's Story supports the idea that anarchists must build alternative institutions that render capitalist institutions superfluous. This vision is similar to the idea of the Black commune that Ervin discusses, as Balagoon was concerned with holding space within the New Afrikan colony. He clearly found that a hierarchical approach would not allow for this, as a commune would constitute a variety of alternative institutions that a single vanguard organization could not simply dictate.

The life of New Afrikan revolutionary and anarchist Kuwasi Balagoon points to critique of hierarchy, embrace of self-determination, and engagement in revolutionary political practice as essential to the work of Black anarchists. Balagoon differs from Ervin in various ways, as his thought relied upon more explicitly anti-colonial and anti-imperialist ideas. While Ervin draws much more from notions of a Black class struggle as applied to the United States, Balagoon focuses on a more international struggle against colonialism and imperialism. While we think that Balagoon's and Ervin's conclusions regarding political practice and conditions are similar, the frameworks are different. Balagoon's theorization of a New Afrikan anarchist is critical as Ervin does not describe himself as New Afrikan but instead as

Black. Balagoon's name change indicates how he was much more in touch with an international Pan-Africanist or African internationalist focus. As we will see, these ideas influenced Black anarchists of the second wave in how they defined the Black struggle in relation to the United States and racial capitalism.

FIRST WAVE CONCLUDED

The first Black anarchist wave is defined principally through their relationships with and critiques of the Black liberation movement. Theorists like Lorenzo Kom'boa Ervin and Kuwasi Balagoon provide a basis for the next wave of Black anarchists. The Black anarchism emerging from the prison struggles, guerrilla struggles, and engagement with anarchist texts during incarceration informed the next wave of Black anarchists. They emphasized Black feminism while continuing to critique the state, authoritarianism, and European-North American anarchism.

ASHANTI ALSTON:
A LINK BETWEEN THE FIRST AND SECOND WAVES

ASHANTI ALSTON

Ashanti Alston's contributions to the Black anarchist theoretical trajectory are significant partly because his writings bridge the first and second waves. Alston is not unique in this bridging. For example, in interviews, Lorenzo Kom'boa Ervin interacted and engaged with theorists from the second wave, such as William C. Anderson. However, Alston's writings and actions incorporated different radical traditions such as queer theory, feminism, and the Zapatistas. In addition, Alston explicitly references other Black anarchist theorists such as Kuwasi Balagoon, as Ervin discussed Martin Sostre.

Also a member of the Black Liberation Army, Alston came from a small town, Plainfield, New Jersey, where a Black rebellion erupted against the white power structure in 1967. Alston describes the importance of Black nationalism to these rebellions in the 1960s. He discusses how "I don't remember when he got assassinated, but it was '65 so I had to be like ten, eleven years old. But '67, there's the rebellions all over the United States, and I know that Malcolm's words were really big" (Alston, 2010:23).

Alston emphasizes the importance of Black nationalism in his work "Beyond Nationalism but Not Without It." In this text, Alston describes:

> Because of the totally racist, genocidal dynamic within this Babylonian Empire, the Black nationalist understood that we must primarily look to ourselves to free ourselves. And none of these thinkers felt it was necessary to "check in" with White Man – from the ruler to the revolutionary – to see if it was okay. It was about our survival as a people, not as that mythical "working class" or that equally mythical "citizen" (Alston, 2004:1).

Alston points to the importance of the Black nationalist thinkers who did not feel the need to get the approval of the white man regardless if the white man was a "ruler or revolutionary." This Black nationalist sensibility is a clear pattern throughout most Black anarchist writing in its opposition to white supremacy and white radicalism.

To Alston, Black nationalist politics are about Black survival, and Black anarchist politics should be in the same tradition. Alston clarifies:

> Anarchism and nationalism are similar in that they are both anti-statist, but what does it mean when the specific anarchist movements within a specific country are racist and dismissive of any and all nationalism, be it reactionary or revolutionary? For me, even the nationalism of a Louis Farrakhan is about saving our people, though it is also thoroughly sexist, capitalist, homophobic and potentially fascist. Yet, it has played an important part in keeping a certain Black pride and resistance going" (Alston, 2004:2).

As Alston describes it, Farrakhan's nationalism, although it is "potentially fascist," has more relevance to the Black struggle than anarchism during the current moment in terms of material knowledge and "saving our people." He contrasts this with racist white anarchists from the European-North American tradition who demean all forms of nationalism regardless of its revolutionary

ASHANTI ALSTON FAMILY PHOTO

or reactionary forms. Alston's reference to Farrakhan points to how a variety of influences shaped his politics. We will continue to focus on these various influences, including feminism and Pan-Africanism.

While other theorists in the first wave, such as Balagoon, Ervin, or Sostre, do not neglect Pan-Africanism, Alston makes explicit reference to his anarchist influences emerging from the African continent:

> I was encouraged by things I found in Africa – not so much by the ancient forms that we call tribes – but by modern struggles that occurred in Zimbabwe, Angola, Mozambique, and Guinea-Bissau. Even though they were led by vanguardist organizations, I saw that people were building radical, democratic communities on the ground. For the first time, in these colonial situations, African peoples where creating what the Angolans called "popular power." ... popular power took a very anti-authoritarian form: people were not only conducting their lives, but also transforming them while fighting whatever foreign power was oppressing them (Alston, 2010:26).

He describes being influenced by the ongoing anti-colonial revolutions occurring in Africa. Alston embraces the vanguardist movements while pointing out that these movements are not homogenous in terms of organizational practice. Despite the vanguardist tendencies, there are many teachings that Black anarchist politics can learn from the "popular power" developed in these anti-colonial revolts. Some from the European-North American anarchist tendency may decry the authoritarianism of the African anti-colonial movements while not fully understanding the scope of these movements. Additionally, Alston's focus, particularly on Africa, sets him apart from other Black anarchists who are more US-centric. Alston's orientation focusing on anti-colonial struggles resembles Balagoon's New Afrikan nationalism, although Alston frames it differently in locating anti-authoritarian currents within anti-colonial movements. In some ways, Alston's explicit overtures toward a Pan-African connection precedes and anticipates *The Anarkata Statement*, which is similar in its orientation towards African anti-colonial politics as an inspiration.

Alston also links the first and second waves by his explicit connection to feminism and queer politics. In one of his interviews, Alston critiques Malcolm X as a revolutionary through a feminist lens. He links this analysis explicitly to anarchism as a political practice that situates the social struggle as important as the political struggle: "I want people to be critical of that so that even in our relationships I want people to see how important our personal, family, social relationships are, because we didn't do that well back then and that played a part on weakening our power as a movement, as an organization" (Alston, 2010:34). During the 1960s and 1970s, Alston notes, Black revolutionaries sometimes did not understand the importance of "personal, family and social" relationships. This problem calls for more feminist politics, which position the transformation of social relationships in our personal lives as revolutionary. Alston points to a weakening of movements without an explicit feminist critique. While other Black anarchists share this position, Alston is the most explicit about it in his interviews and zines.

In another interview he talks about his engagement with queer theory:

> I said something to her [a queer comrade] one day kind of innocently but it was really fucked up, so homophobic. So she said, Ashanti I've got something I want you to read. So the next day we're going to work and she gives me this book Queer Theory and it's like, queer theory! I have struggled to be a good ally but now she's asking me to read this book. So I am on the subway with this book (laughing). I am so conscious that I have this highly charged title and so I don't hold the book like I do normally, I reading it like this (holds the book cover down), now I'm holding it down so people can't see the title and I'm conscious of myself doing that (Alston, 2010:30).

Alston's personal relationship with his queer comrade sparks him to engage with queer theory. We see a resonance here with the Black feminist sensibility that the personal is political and that radical struggle occurs in every aspect of our lives.

This is an important bridge for Black anarchist theoretical development. Alston's explicit mention of these politics serves as a prelude for the later contributions of the Anarkatas and Samudzi as they incorporate Black feminist and Black queer politics. In Alston's analysis, he joins the anti-colonial struggle to struggles in personal lives around gender especially. He states how he began to understand:

> our struggle outside of me but how those struggles are inside of me as well. Those intersections that you are talking about now (race, class, gender). But for me, too, I never put aside the anti-colonial perspective because for me, our struggle in the United States, especially for people of African descent, we're still in an anti-colonial struggle (Alston, 2010:30).

In this way, Alston joins anti-authoritarian, anti-oppressive, and anti-colonial politics.

These multiple influences in his writing also serve as a critique of European-North American anarchist orthodoxy. Alston makes the criticism that:

> Anarchist theory and practice cannot take the form of a mere adherence to the founding fathers and canonical practices, such as Kropotkin, Bakunin, and the Spanish Civil War. Tired of hearing it! Anarchism HERE in Babylon must reflect our unique problems and possibilities for struggle. Our struggles are not just against capitalism. Too simple. Our struggles are not just against racism. That's also too simple. There are all kinds of negative "isms" we are fighting against and, just as important, all kinds of worlds we are fighting for (Alston 2004:3).

Like Ervin and Balagoon, Alston situates his Black anarchism within a struggle against "Babylon" or the U.S. empire. Alston emphasizes that struggle in the United States will have to reflect the conditions and realities here. This is something that both Balagoon and Ervin describe, especially in their different approaches to nationalism and their critiques of the white left. According to Alston, the struggle is not just against capitalism or racism but rather all sorts of negative "ism(s)." This speaks to his concern with confronting all sorts of oppressive behavior. In general, Alston blends several ideologies and influences that resonate with *The Anarkata Statement*, to which we return later.

For example, a quote in "Beyond Nationalism But Not Without It" shows the range of influences from the Black radical tradition from which he draws:

> Ella Baker said we can do it if we can trust ourselves and get away from leadership-led revolution; Kuwasi Balagoon said we can do it if we are willing to create a chaos that will shut this mutha down; Audre Lorde said we can do it if we LEARN TO LOVE AND RESPECT OUR BEAUTIFUL DIVERSITY and reject the tools of our oppressors; Harriet Tubman said ain't a better way to live THAN

AT-WAR FOR A RIGHTEOUS CAUSE; and Franz Fanon said if we smack that mutha across the face, drive that pig out from our territory at the point of a gun, it IS LIBERATING FOR THE SOUL (Alston, 2004:3).

Here Alston refers to anti-colonial and anti-oppressive theoretical influences as well as people who, apart from Frantz Fanon (though his influence on Black radicals is unquestionable), are essential parts of Black radical history in the United States. Baker, Lorde, and Tubman are examples of Alston's focus on Black women in struggle. Both Baker and Lorde questioned power in social movement spaces, especially around gender, and tried to break it down at all levels. While neither identified as an anarchist, it is easy to see how they influenced Black anarchists like Alston. Additionally, Alston makes his militant abolitionism known with references to Balagoon and Tubman. Finally, his reference to Fanon resonates with his reference to Balagoon because the struggle is ultimately anti-colonial and will require driving the repressive forces from the land. Alston's dedication to principles of anti-colonialist and anti-oppressive politics lives on in the second wave of Black anarchist politics.

Chapter 5
The Second Wave of Black Anarchism

The second wave emerged from social movements in the 2010s. Black rebellions in Ferguson and Baltimore, the resurgent anti-fascist movement, the prison abolitionists, and Occupy all provided the basis for coalescing. A renewed interest in Black anarchist politics came from these struggles. Much of the writing happened in prisons and during moments of reassessment when Black radical movements were in abeyance. Anarchistic ideas have permeated Black radical movements and discourse within these movements.

We focus on texts concerning the intersection of Black radical politics and anarchy. Primary texts include *As Black as Resistance* by Zoé Samudzi and William C. Anderson (2018) and *The Anarkata Statement* published by Afrofuturist Abolitionists of the Americas (2019). These texts come from the Black radical tradition while not engaging with the U.S. anarchist canon. In addition, both texts refer to the prior wave of Black anarchists. The second wave is like the first wave as the theorists are operating, for the most part, independently from one another. The text *As Black as Resistance* and *The Anarkata Statement* are vastly different and relatively unconnected. However, they share ideological influences relating to the ideas around abolition, queer traditions, Black radicalism, and prior Black anarchists.

ZOÉ SAMUDZI AND WILLIAM C. ANDERSON: ANARCHISM OF BLACKNESS

As Black as Resistance by Samudzi and Anderson articulates Black anarchism through a more explicitly Black feminist perspective. It comes less from an explicit critique of revolutionary nationalist organizing structures than from the social movements of the 2010s, with the flowering of Afro-pessimist writing, the work of eco-feminists, anti-colonial theorists, and further contributions by prior Black anarchists. This text does not explicitly name any classical European or North American anarchist theorists but instead relies more upon decades of Black radical scholarship and history.

However, we distinguish this text from the work of Black anarchists like Lorenzo Kom'boa Ervin and Kuwasi Balagoon. Ervin and Balagoon were much more rooted in their active involvement with the Panthers and the BLA and their experiences as political prisoners. This articulation of Black anarchism is mostly a product of the prison-industrial complex (PIC) abolition movement.

The book begins with an introduction by Mariame Kaba. As a well-known prison abolitionist organizer, Kaba articulates the resonances:

ZOÉ SAMUDZI

> In that respect, abolitionism and anarchism are positive rather than negative projects. They do not signal the absence of prisons or governments but the creation of different forms of sociality, governance, and accountability that are not statist and carceral (Kaba in Samudzi and Anderson, 2018:xvii-xviii).

She begins by describing anarchism and abolitionism as linked projects that are positive rather than negative. The links between abolitionism and anarchism are projects building a new world without the state locating how these ideologies could be understood as in affinity. Ideologically, abolitionism comes from the Black radical tradition and Black feminism, with seminal abolitionist texts, *Are Prisons Obsolete?* by Angela Davis and *Golden Gulag* by Ruth Wilson Gilmore. These two authors were among the activists and scholars who founded the abolitionist organization Critical Resistance. The PIC abolition movement emerged because the PIC is explicitly linked to the capture of Black political prisoners such as Balagoon, Alston, and Ervin, who all subsequently became anarchists. Beginning the text with an introduction by Kaba situates *As Black as Resistance* as an abolitionist text. Samudzi and Anderson's *Black Anarchism* is grounded in abolitionism.

They make a distinction between their analysis and that of the first wave:

> Black Americans are residents of a settler colony, not truly citizens of the United States…. The Black American condition today is an evolved condition directly connected to this history of slavery, and that will continue to be the case as long as the United States remains as an ongoing settler project (Samudzi and Anderson, 2018:8).

Describing Black people in the United States as "Black Americans" departs from a New Afrikan or even an African identity. Later on, the authors critique Black nationalists in the United States for voiding the sovereignty of nation-states in Africa while at the same moment criticizing formations such as the Republic of New Afrika for engaging in almost a Black zionist politic. The authors argue that the condition of African slave descendants will continue to be linked to slavery as long as the United States remains a settler-colonial project.

WILLIAM C. ANDERSON

Making explicit reference to settler-colonialism departs from the "internal colony" thesis or a theory about Black people in the United States as "colonized." As Black as Resistance focuses on the relationship of Black people to the state throughout the history of slavery. They argue that Black people will never be accepted as citizens of the United States because the country is built on the exclusion of Black people from the social contract. Samudzi and Anderson state that "we are Black because we are oppressed by the state; we are oppressed by the state because we are Black" (2018:9).

This situation is where they find their aspirations towards Black anarchism. They locate the relationship of Black people to the state as "blackening through subjugation" and declare that the Black identity cannot be positively re-asserted. At the end of the book, they say:

> Commentary about the anarchistic nature of blackness is not necessarily advocacy for anarchist politics or ideology. Instead, it describes a condition that might lend itself to a form of organization reflecting that tendency. Blackness itself is anarchistic as a result of Black exclusion from the social contract (and thus non-assimilation into the state) (2018:109).

Samudzi and Anderson's Black anarchism theorizes a relationship of Black people to the state and then understands the necessity of an anti-state politic.

The anarchism in this text is slightly different from the Black anarchism articulated by Ervin or Balagoon, which was more an evolution of tactics and organizational structure after the failures of the Black liberation movement during the 1960s and 1970s. Nevertheless, the authors explicitly reference Ervin's work, taking inspiration from Black anarchism. They say:

> While we may not choose to limit or misrepresent the diversity of our struggle by explicitly naming ourselves as "anarchists", we should nevertheless cultivate an internationalist framework and draw inspiration from movements for sovereignty and autonomy both domestically and globally (Samudzi and Anderson, 2018:66).

After describing the need for autonomist politics, they reference a section from *Anarchism and the Black Revolution*, where Ervin discusses the need for dual power in collective and communal models of organization.

However, rather than explicitly naming themselves as anarchists with the addition of a signifier such as Black or New Afrikan, the authors seek to cultivate a politics of autonomy by taking inspiration from the work of Black anarchists like Ervin. The authors are less interested in being anarchists than in finding politics that work. They view Ervin's organizing model as important because it veers away from hierarchies, cults of personality, and centralized leadership structures. They critique Ervin by mentioning how it is not enough to "simply center blackness in our understanding of resistance to subjugation" (Samudzi and Anderson, 2018:68). According to the authors, "Any truly liberatory politics must speak to the unique needs and vulnerability of Black women and girls, particularly Black Queer and transgender women and girls" (2018:68). Their statement follows after they reference two sections of Ervin's book *Anarchism and the Black Revolution*. This part of the text was meant to critique and extend Ervin's work.

Samudzi and Anderson also refer to Ervin when discussing self-defense in Black movements. Specifically, they reference a section in *Anarchism and the Black Revolution* where Ervin critiques the Black Panther Party for "small group terrorism and adventurism" regarding guns as props. Samudzi and Anderson resonate with Ervin's criticism of vanguard parties, especially concerning the use of force. But instead, Samudzi and Anderson propose a mass movement that would not fetishize the use of guns. They describe how gun violence is linked to domestic and intimate partner violence. Again, this moment is an example of how the second wave of Black anarchists built upon the theory created by the first wave of Black anarchists. Often, they augment it with queer or Black feminist methodologies.

They discuss the oppression of the Black woman as it relates to the anarchistic nature of blackness. Black feminist theory influenced this idea. Samudzi and Anderson argue:

> Black feminism responds to the racist exclusion of Black women from "women's issues"– safety, deservedness, agency and autonomy,

and classed oppression. Understanding Black women's subjugation by the state means understanding raced and gendered labor extraction, and Black feminism is useful for understanding the functioning of capitalism and for undermining the legitimacy of this anti-Black settler state (2018:53),

Black feminism analyzes Black subjugation by the state and particularly how it affects Black women. Engagement with Black feminism as anarchistic remains a common theme within the second wave of Black anarchist politics. The exclusion of Black women from movements for bodily autonomy places a new dimension into Black anarchic politics. This trend continues and deepens with *The Anarkata Statement*. However, these pieces were created in different moments and from diverse ideological backgrounds, even as they both reference anarchists such as Ervin.

ANARKATA:
PAN-AFRICAN ANARCHIST POLITICS

ANARKATA STATEMENT

The Anarkata Statement published in 2019 is a Black anarchist statement or manifesto detailing "anarkata" politics. The Statement differs from *As Black as Resistance* as it is not issued by any identifiable persons. The authors are anonymous. The first distribution of *The Anarkata Statement* was published and disseminated on the Afrofuturist Abolitionists of the Americas WordPress page. This organization is a self-described "collective of revolutionaries within the Black freedom struggle and Afrikan liberation efforts, who bring a speculative vibe to our radical work" (afanarchists.com). The document states that it is:

> ...not to be a founding document for one particular organization but is intended to be a jumping off point for anarchic Black radicals to cohere our diverse thoughts together. The authors have not written this to speak for all things in anarchic Black revolution, but we write this as an invitation to us all to put our heads and minds together (2019:4).

The Anarkata Statement does not position itself as the sole expression of the Black anarchist tendency but rather as the confluence of several ideological traditions. Various ideological traditions have always been an essential element of Black anarchist thought.

The authors locate themselves in reaction to two different tendencies and some other influences. According to the *Statement*,

> "Anarkata" emerges as a response to the political alienation that has been experienced by Black anarcho adjacent leftists who reject both the whiteness of traditional anarchism and the authoritarianism of some forms of Black nationalism (2019:3).

That *The Anarkata Statement* has emerged partly from alienation to the whiteness of traditional anarchism resonates with the work of Ervin, Alston, and Sostre, continuing a long theme within Black anarchist writing that understands white anarchism and anarchists as insufficient.

The *Statement*'s explicit comment about the whiteness of traditional anarchism contrasts with *As Black as Resistance*, which does not engage with the whiteness of traditional anarchism. Describing the relationship between European-North American anarchism and their own tendency, the authors describe how they "find ourselves overlooked, and our politics get confused and dismissed as synonymous with classical, European Anarchism...often misunderstood by the non-anarchic world as largely an aesthetic and utopian movement" (2019:3).

The critiques of traditional anarchism, while not expanded upon within the Statement, provide a partial basis for the Anarkata to distinguish themselves from non-Black anarchists and act in the revolutionary tradition of self-naming. The term is short for "anarchic akata," which reclaims the Yoruba term "housecat" or "wild animal" (2019:3). The term Akata is a slur, so the term must remain only used by Black people. Furthermore, there is an implication that we should respect any Black person who does not wish to be called Anarkata. This issue of naming is similar to Ervin's naming himself a Black autonomist or Balagoon's naming himself a "New Afrikan anarchist." In all situations, these Black anarchists differentiate themselves from European-North American anarchist traditions. The Anarkatas draw themselves into conflict with the authoritarian forms of Black nationalism, which resonates within the work of Black anarchists. This is distinct from *As Black as Resistance*, as the Anarkata text is not attempting to discuss blackness in relation to the state as explicitly as Samudzi and Anderson's idea of "the anarchistic nature of blackness." Similar to Ervin and Balagoon howe, they do not outright reject Black nationalism.

The authors later detail their tendency's reaction to authoritarianism with explicit reference to Ervin's work:

> Absolute, uncritical loyalty to the mandates of a political organization and its leadership (even after a "democratic" decision-making process) is not "principled" or "disciplined" but authoritarian and dangerous. As Black anarchist Lorenzo Kom'boa Ervin pointed out, "democratic centralism poses as a form of inner party democracy, but is really just a hierarchy by which each member of a party is subordinate to a higher member (2019:18).

The *Statement* distinguishes itself from authoritarian formations by describing how being uncritical of a political organization and the leadership is not "principled." The statement locates anti-authoritarianism taking root in the structures of leadership within organizations. From the reference to Ervin, it is clear that the Anarkatas oppose the hierarchy of inner party democracy.

This engagement with organizational form speaks to how *The Anarkata Statement* is a text inspired through and through by movement work. The nod to Ervin comes from the fact that the people engaging with his work had been involved with Ervin's theoretical and organizational writing. Similarly again to Ervin and Balagoon, they are still sympathetic to Black nationalism in some forms. The Statement says that "we recognize the unifying role of Black nationalism in anti-colonial movements and affirm that the continuing debate around our way forward must be worked out among ourselves without any interference from non-Black people" (2019:6). This affirmation of Black nationalism as "unifying" rings similar to Balagoon's and Ervin's statements about nationalism. However, the Statement differs as it makes explicit references to an anarchist Pan-Africanism, which is something not addressed in prior Black anarchist writing. That writing focused intensely on the experiences of Black people in the United States. However, the discussion of Pan-Africanism is not surprising as references to Black nationalism and Africa occur in much prior Black anarchist writing.

The Anarkata Statement names Pan-Africanism as an explicit part of its politics. This is interesting considering that Pan-Africanism as an ideology emerged initially from a nation-state oriented politics. The Anarkatas describe:

> Pan-Africanism connects Anarkata struggles for freedom to all members of the African community including the diaspora, understanding Black liberation outside the confines of national borders, and tying our bodily freedom to the liberation of our entire

homeland itself from the snares of neocolonial/military-imperial rule (2019:5).

The idea that Pan-Africanism is a way to understand Black liberation outside borders falls in line with Anarkata's resistance to enclosure of land to transfer it from a resource shared in common to a piece of private property.

Tying to the African homeland explicitly is key as the *Statement* names the connection to Africa, which is implicit in much of Black anarchist writing while not appearing explicitly as a value. The Statement references the work of African anarchist Sam Mbah, as well as the history of mutual aid as African in origin:

> … we understand mutual aid as an African method of collective support for our communities that Black people have practiced since precolonial times. It involves the distribution of money, food, water, services, skills, medical care, shelter, and other necessities to those who require them" (2019:15).

The Anarkata Statement links an anarchist method of organization to a pre-colonial African tradition, identifying the politics as Pan-African in orientation and therefore setting it apart from other Black anarchist thought. Through an explicit reference to mutual aid as an African method, the authors emphasize the importance of pre-colonial Africa as *The Anarkata Statement* traces its legacy further back than Black resistance to slavery in the United States but rather to African lifeways on the continent. This orientation distinguishes the Anarkata from some forms of Black radicalism that do not embrace African history.

Despite the similarities to the first wave of Black anarchism when it refers to European-North American anarchism and Black nationalism, *The Anarkata Statement* departs in meaningful ways, especially about the politics of the body. By references to Black feminism, queer and trans liberation, and disability justice, the Anarkatas theorize their ideological commitments as against all forms of hierarchy:

> Anarkatas believe that all hierarchies subject Black people to forms of capture, captivity, and commodification. Due to the historical processes of African enslavement that marked and transformed African bodies into property, chattel, and non-human merchandise, Black people have a particular vulnerability to captivity that is anchored by our bodies being marked as inhuman (2019:5).

The Anarkatas do not describe hierarchies as primarily a part of a larger class struggle, struggle against settler-colonialism, or struggle against imperialism. Instead, the Anarkata analysis comes out explicitly against all forms of domination, while this critique remains implicit in many of the prior Black anarchist texts that we have connected. In addition, *The Anarkata Statement* describes the historical process of slavery to understand how African people were transformed into "property, chattel, and non-human merchandise."

The Anarkatas go on to describe that "white supremacy, ableism, cisheterosexism, capitalism, colonialism, humanism, misogynoir, transmisogynoir, and patriarchy consist of hierarchical layers of power that place Black people in continued positions of vulnerability to capture, enslavement, and death..." (2019:5). This statement's explicit analysis, which opposes all forms of hierarchy in relation to Black subjugation, makes it distinct from other forms of Black anarchist politics. At the root of the politics according to the statement is the "Black tendency to defy rigidity, borders, hierarchy, and enclosure..." (2019:4). The Anarkatas understand Black cultures of oppositionalism and non-hierarchical organization as anarchistic. They make explicit reference to the work of Panther anarchist Ashanti Alston where he describes, "when we speak of a Black anarchism, it is not so tied to the color of our skin but who I am as a person, as someone who can resist, who can see differently when I am stuck, and thus live differently" (2019:3). The idea of Black cultures of opposition as anarchic is distinct from the prior works that we have engaged. Ultimately, a "synthesis of Black radical oppositionalities, along the lines of a Black nonhierarchical critique" (2019:4), locates a Black anarchism grounded in Black radical politics, history, and life, rather than a non-Black position centered in Europe and North America.

The Anarkata Statement is emblematic of the new wave of Black anarchists as they draw from a variety of influences. While *As Black as Resistance* discusses Black feminist theory, *The Anarkata Statement* engages with Black feminism, Pan-Africanism, and disability as a part of the Statement's Black anarchist analytic. Black feminism is apparent throughout the entire text, with a continuing reference to bodily autonomy and engagement with different types of oppressions.

> Black feminism has provided the critical lens for Anarkatas to understand how our oppressions as Black people intersect to leave some at the margins and very bottom of hierarchy, teaching us to center the overlooked and extremely vulnerable; Queer/trans liberation has taught Anarkatas to re-envision the way we inhabit and understand our bodies as Black people, beyond sexual and anatomical reductions forced onto us by colonialism and capitalism (2019:4).

Black feminism and queer liberation are clearly core parts of the Anarkata tradition. The text makes multiple references to STAR, a revolutionary trans organization. A*s Black as Resistance* mentioned, the importance of understanding how oppressions intersect; however, within *The Anarkata Statement* in the section "Anarkata politics," the writers analyze extensively the systems of misogynoir, misogyny directed toward Black women, and especially trans-misogynoir.

The racialized nature of gender and the oppression of Black women in racial capitalist society and in revolutionary movements become central concerns of the Anarkatas. The writers understand gender as a "colonial imposition," which directly affects Black people in general but specifically subjects Black trans women and all non-men to abuses by men. The Statement links queer liberation to a project aiming to destroy colonialism (2019:9).

Ableism is another essential part of the Anarkata framework, not mentioned within any other Black anarchist writing. *The Anarkata Statement* links disability justice to "the bodily autonomy of our people outside of slavery and imperialism" (2019:13). A necessity that a Black liberation politic centers disabled Black people is a new contribution to Black anarchist theorization. *The Anarkata Statement* reframes disability justice as it "can come from us, not the State" (2019:13). Delinking disability justice from the state further emphasizes how the politics of the body have become even more essential within the second wave of Black anarchist writing. In contrast to other Black anarchist writing, Anarkata politics emphasize liberation of the Black body as a site of resistance.

Furthermore, *The Anarkata Statement* expands upon ideas in anarchism about bottom-up self-organization. The *Statement* describes how "Anarkatas say that disability justice is ultimately about people power in its clearest sense, and see it as central to all of the political positions we espouse here." In regard to people power, the *Statement* focuses on how to foster power from the bottom up, as Black anarchist politics reverse the marginalization of disabled people. Emphasis on the politics of disability justice is critical within *The Anarkata Statement* and signals a major departure from the first wave of Black anarchist political thought.

Ultimately, while drawing from Black anarchists of the past, *The Anarkata Statement* applies multiple different sources and deepens the group's revolutionary politics. *The Anarkata Statement* represents the furthest evolution of Black anarchist politics that continue to embrace a critique of all systems of power while remaining rooted in Black struggle. The second wave of Black anarchism contributes new politics with attention to abolition and Black feminism. This wave does not attempt to critique the European-North American anarchist movements but rather presents a new approach to politics inspired by Ferguson and the Baltimore uprisings.

The two distinct waves of Black anarchist theorization provide a basis for understanding how Black radicals who either identify explicitly as anarchists or share affinity with anarchism are not doing so in a way oriented toward prior anarchist traditions. Instead, while it applies certain concepts from prior anarchist traditions, Black anarchism engages mainly with a Black radical tradition that emphasizes a revolutionary transformation of racial capitalism.

Chapter 6
Conclusion:
Toward Black Autonomy

And now the fires are settling. The rebellion has ended. We see politicians and their calls, which range from #DefundThePolice to #BackTheBlue. Meanwhile, the coronavirus continues to ravage Black communities despite hopes for vaccines and the Biden presidency. So we return to the questions from the beginning. Where are the Black anarchists? Why does Black anarchism matter?

It matters because, from this point on, the course of Black radicalism cannot be understood adequately without Black anarchism. Furthermore, if anarchists from the European-North American tradition, as well as all other people struggling to overcome racial capitalism, want to be relevant to social struggles, they need to study and support the work of Black anarchists.

We have argued that the relationship between anarchism and the Black radical tradition has been contentious. We looked at the history of European-North American anarchism and emphasized weaknesses of class reductionism and inadequate analysis of racial capitalism; the U.S. anarchist milieu has not grappled adequately with the interrelations of race and class. Finally, we described the emergence of two waves of Black anarchism. We explained how these Black anarchist politics grew from the Black radical tradition rather than the European-North American anarchist canon. Black anarchist politics, we argued, have centered around a resistance to racial capitalism and the conjuncture of racial and class oppression. We discussed the differences between the first wave, composed mostly of former Panthers and Black nationalists, and the second wave, taking more influence from Black feminism, abolitionism, and several other frameworks.

Study of Black anarchism and anarchistic forms of Black radicalism should continue. For instance, the relationships between prison organizing and Black anarchism need clarification. During our work, we encountered writing from a number of incarcerated Black anarchists, such as Hybachi Lemar and Michael Kimble. These writers need to be investigated and better understood. More work should focus on the history and development of the Black Autonomy Federation, as well as other explicitly Black anarchist formations. There needs to be more writing about anarchistic politics within Black radical movements. We have focused on individuals who identify as Black, radical, and anarchist, but many radical movements and theorists do not label themselves as anarchists for reasons that future study about Black anarchism should consider. Finally, there needs to be more research and theorizing about the intersections of Black anarchism and anarcho-feminism. Other than some of Zoé Samudzi's lectures and the work of the Anarkatas, little work has engaged questions about Black radical feminism and Black anarchism. Most well-known theorists of Black anarchist politics continue to be cis and male. Black anarchist politics includes a wide breadth of topics just waiting to be explored.

Recently, Lorenzo Kom'boa Ervin did an interview facilitated by William C. Anderson, two theorists whose work we engaged in this text. During the interview, Ervin discussed how uprisings have limits. He argued that anarchists need to build "ungovernable communities." Additionally, Ervin acknowledged just recently learning about exciting new tendencies within Black anarchism. He gives a brief history of the Black Autonomy Federation, an organization that he formed in the 1990s. Black anarchism continues to grow and to change in our current moment.

During and after the 2020 uprising, these two Black anarchists have discussed what a world beyond capitalism could look like. This is where radical movements must focus. More than ever, interest in Black anarchism is growing. To witness two members from the different Black anarchist waves interacting is encouraging as it pictures the future of Black revolutionary politics. Such contributions of Black anarchist politics will be vital towards building a more liberated post-capitalist world.

References

Abolitionfuturist. (2019). "Anarkata: A Statement." *The Anarkata Statement.* https://anarkataastatement.wordpress.com/.

Alston [Omowali], Ashanti. (2001). "On Kuwasi Balagoon." http://www.revoltlib.com/anarchism/on-kuwasi-balagoon-alston-ashanti/.

Alston, Ashanti. (2004). "Beyond Nationalism But Not Without It." Oakland, CA: Jailbreak Press. https://archive.org/details/jailbreak_2004_beyond_nationalism

Alston, Ashanti, with Hilary Darcy. (2010). "Be Careful of Your Man-Tones! Gender Politics in Revolutionary Struggle." *Interface: a journal for and about social movements.* Activist interview. 2 (1): 22-35. http://www.interfacejournal.net/wordpress/wp-content/uploads/2010/11/Interface-2-1-pp22-35-Alston.pdf.

Balagoon, Kuwasi. (1983). "Brink's Trial Opening Statement," July 11, 1983. https://usa.anarchistlibraries.net/library/kuwasi-balagoon-brink-s-trial-opening-statement.pdf.

Balagoon, Kuwasi. (2012). "Anarchy Can't Fight Alone." https://libcom.org/library/anarchy-cant-fight-alone.

Balagoon, Kuwasi. (2019). *A Soldier's Story: Revolutionary Writings by a New Afrikan Anarchist.* Edited by Matt Meyer and Karl Kersplebedeb. Oakland, CA: PM Press.

Bookchin, Murray. (1995). *Social Anarchism or Lifestyle Anarchism: An Unbridgeable Chasm.* Chico, CA: AK Press.

Ciccarello-Maher, George. (2011). "An anarchism that is not anarchism: notes towards a critique of anarchist imperialism," in J.C. Klausen and J. Martel (eds.). How Not To Be Governed. Lanham, MD: Lexington Books.

Cornell, Andrew. (2016). *Unruly Equality: US Anarchism in the Twentieth Century.* Oakland, CA: University of California Press.

Dixon, Chris. (2012). "Building Another Politics: The Contemporary Anti-Authoritarian Current in the US and Canada." Anarchist Studies 20.1.

Ervin, Lorenzo Kom'boa. (1993). *Anarchism and the Black Revolution: The Idea of Black Autonomy.* N.P.: P & L Printing.

Ervin, Lorenzo Kom'boa. (2011). *The Progressive Plantation: Racism inside White Radical Social Change Organizations.* Chicago, IL: True Leap Press & Distribution.

Ervin, Lorenzo. (2020). "Martin Sostre: Prison Revolutionary." Black Rose/Rosa Negra Anarchist Federation. https://blackrosefed.org/martin-sostre-prison-revolutionary-komboa/.

Ervin, Lorenzo Kom'boa and JoNina Abron. (2000). "Black Autonomy: Civil Rights, the Panthers and Today." https://libcom.org/library/Black-autonomy-civil-rights-the-panthers-and-today.

Fanon, Frantz. (1963). *The Wretched of the Earth*. New York: Grove.
Ferguson, Kathy E. (2013). *Emma Goldman: Political Thinking in the Streets*. Lanham, MD: Rowman & Littlefield Publishers.
Graeber, David. (2010) *Direct Action: An Ethnography*. Chico, CA: AK Press.
Heynen, Nik, and Jason Rhodes. (2014). 1. "Organizing for Survival: From the Civil Rights Movement to Black Anarchism through the Life of Lorenzo Kom'boa Ervin." *ACME: An International Journal for Critical Geographies* 11 (3), 393-412. https://acme-journal.org/index.php/acme/article/view/939.
Johnson, Greg. (1996). "Authoritarian Leftists: Kill the Cop in Your Head." *Industrial Workers of the World*. https://iww.org/history/library/Ervin/copinyourhead.
Mbah, Sam, and I. E. Igariwey, *African Anarchism: The History of a Movement*. Tucson, AZ: See Start Press, 1997.
Olson, Joel (2009). "Between Infoshops and Insurrection: U.S. Anarchism, Movement Building, and the Racial Order." https://blackrosefed.org/between-infoshops-and-insurrection-olson/.
Perry, Lewis. (1996). *Radical Abolitionism: Anarchy and the Government of God in Antislavery Thought*. Knoxville: University of Tennessee Press.
Robinson, Cedric. (2000). *Black Marxism: The Making of the Black Radical Tradition*. Chapel Hill, N.C: University of North Carolina Press.
Robinson, Cedric. (2016). *The Terms of Order*. Chapel Hill, N.C: University of North Carolina Press.
Reedier, David. (2016). *Seizing Freedom: Slave Emancipation and Liberty for All*. London, UK: Verso.
Samudzi, Zoé, and William C. Anderson. (2018). *As Black as Resistance: Finding the Conditions for Liberation*. Chico, CA: AK Press.
Shone, Steve J. (2010). *Lysander Spooner: American Anarchist*. Lanham, MD: Lexington Books.
Sunshine, Spencer. (2013). *Post-1960 U.S. anarchism and social theory*. PhD Dissertation. New York: City University of New York. https://www.worldcat.org/title/post-1960-us-anarchism-and-social-theory/oclc/873626873.
Ture, Kwame, and Charles V. Hamilton. *Black Power: The Politics of Liberation in America*. New York: Random House, 1967.
Umoja, Akinyele K. (2015). "Maroon: Kuwasi Balagoon and the Evolution of Revolutionary New Afrikan Anarchism." *Science & Society* 79(2): 196–220. doi: 10.1521/siso.2015.79.2.196.
Van der Walt, Lucien, and Michael Schmidt. 2009. *Black Flame: the Revolutionary Class Politics of Anarchism and Syndicalism*. Edinburgh: AK Press.
Washington, Albert Nuh. (1986). "On Kuwasi Balagoon." http://www.revoltlib.com/anarchism/on-kuwasi-balagoon-alston-ashanti/.

Williams, Dana M. (2015). "Black Panther Radical Factionalization and the Development of Black Anarchism." *Journal of Black Studies* 46(7): 678–703. www.jstor.org/stable/24572914.

Woodcock, George. (1962). *Anarchism: A History of Libertarian Ideas and Movements*. Cleveland: The World Publishing Company.

About the Authors & Editors

AUTHORS

Atticus Bagby-Williams is a communist theorist though he likes to think of himself as an anarchist in practice. His theoretical work is concerned with historical and contemporaneous black anarchist thought, the multiplicity of social struggles against oppression in the United States, and third worldist perspectives on revolution. His anarchist practice is concerned primarily with community based radical education, cultivating cultures of community self defense and anti-repression work. He has written for Red Voice and the Commoner and previously published a chapter with Shemon and Arturo in the book The Revolutionary Meaning of the George Floyd Rebellion.

Nsambu (or "Bl3ssing"), Za Suekama: they/she, is a New African woman of nonbinary/transgender experience, focused on revolutionary organizing and educating at the crossroads of Black ecology, Third Worldism, transfeminist materialism, and anarchist/autonomist movement. They previously published "To The Ones Who Can Fly: A Message from the Whirlwind" (True Leap Press), including a study guide for support of Black trans prisoners. Her radical theoretical contributions have been featured on Red Voice News and Afrofuturist Abolitionists of the Americas.

EDITORS

Shannon Fauwkes (they/them) is a non-binary BlaQueer organizer in the Midwest who's current work focuses primarily on abolition, Black Autonomous/Anarchic Radical (BAR) theory and praxis, and creating affordable, cooperative housing options in their city with their co-op crew. They live and work at a Catholic Worker hospitality house for single mothers with children. Shannon is the co-editor of this book and an organizer of the Martin Sostre Solidarity House, in Milwaukee, Wisconsin.

Howard Waitzkin is Distinguished Professor Emeritus of Sociology at the University of New Mexico and practices internal medicine part-time in rural New Mexico and Illinois. For many years he has been active in struggles focusing on health in the United States and Latin America. He is the coordinator, with the Working Group for Health Beyond Capitalism, of Health Care Under the Knife: Moving Beyond Capitalism for Our Health, Monthly Review Press, 2018. He is the editor, with Firoze Manji, of the series: *Moving Beyond Capitalism.*

Titles of Interest from Daraja Press

The Revolutionary Meaning of the George Floyd Uprising
Shemon Salam & Arturo Castillon

A rebellion exploded in Minneapolis in May 2020 in response to the brutal police murder of George Floyd. The uprising quickly spread across the U.S. as protesters fought the police. In an effort to think through the experience of the uprising *The Revolutionary Meaning of the George Floyd Uprising* provides an in-depth analysis of what exactly happened during the 2020 uprising, its potentials, internal limits, and strategic implications.

$15 USD • $20 CAN • 60 pages

Settler Colonialism
Roxanne Dunbar-Ortiz

Settler Colonialism examines the USA as the first full-fledged settler state in the world. The nation of immigrants myth erases the fact that the U.S. was founded as a settler state from its inception and spent years at war against the Native Nations. The text originates from Dunbar-Ortiz (2021) "Not A Nation of Immigrants: Settler Colonialism, White Supremacy, and a History of Erasure and Exclusion."

$20 USD • $27 CAN • 61 pages

A Mutiny of Morning
Nikesha Breeze

Breeze has taken pages from Joseph Conrad's *Heart of Darkness*, taken his words, and forced them to leave his colonized mind. She has made the words her own in poetic form. She illuminates the invisible Black voices inside, a radical, surgical, and unapologetic Black appropriation. The resulting poems are sizzling purifications, violent restorations of integrity, pain, wound, bewilderment, rage, and, sometimes, luminous generosity.

$30 USD • $41 CAN • 164 pages

Mathare: An Urban Bastion of Anti-Oppression Struggle in Kenya
Samuel Gathanga Ndung'u

The story of Mathare Slum in the heart of Nairobi from its role as the planning ground for the Mau Mau struggle in 1963 through the four regimes that have succeeded each other since independence. This book recounts the history of Mathare from an informed insider's perspective by threading the struggles from the colonial era to the present and the role it has played in agitating for social justice.

$20 USD • $27 CAN • 74 pages

Jackson Rising: The Struggle for Economic Democracy and Black Self-Determination in Jackson, Mississippi
Kali Akuno & Ajamu Nangwaya

Mississippi is the poorest state in the U.S. with the highest percentage of Black people and a history of vicious racial terror. The concurrent Black resistance is the backdrop and context for the drama captured in this collection of essays that describe the strategies and methods being pursued by this ongoing movement for Black community control and people-centered economic development.

$20.50 USD • $28 CAN • 312 pages

Racism, Capitalism, and the COVID-19 Pandemic
Zophia Edwards

This piece seeks to understand how the exploitation of Black and other nonwhite racialized labor has persisted throughout the Covid crisis through the lens of Black radical scholarship on racism and capitalism. It historicizes the pandemic within the long arc of racist capitalist labor super-exploitation. It also shows the mechanisms by which Covid has exacerbated already existing, structural racial and colonial inequalities.

$13 USD • $18 CAN • 34 pages

Abolitionist Agroecology, Food Sovereignty and Pandemic Prevention
Maywa Montenegro de Wit

To tackle pandemics and food injustices, Montenegro de Wit calls for an abolitionist agroecology. No anti-capitalist alternative can ignore the racism that is central to the transnational food system. Although abolition is frequently seen as an oppositional strategy, it is equally propositional. An abolitionist agroecology cracks open multiple possibilities that respond to the exigencies of a pandemic planet.

$15 USD • $20 CAN • 79 pages

Moving Beyond Capitalist Agriculture: Could Agroecology Prevent Further Pandemics?
Pandemic Research for the People

A crisis-prone economic system that prioritizes production for profit over human needs and ecological preservation is organized around intense monocultural production that, along the way, allows the deadliest of diseases to emerge. Pandemic Research for the People (PReP) focuses on how agriculture might be reimagined as the kind of community-wide intervention that could stop pathogens from emerging.

$15 USD • $20 CAN • 51 pages

Order from **darajapress.com** or **zandgraphics.com**

Printed and bound in the United Kingdom
09/03/2026
02067239-0001